Trilogy-A
Vol. X

Exile
Trauma
and
Death

On the road to Chankiri with Komitas Vartabed

by

Aram Andonian

Translated,
edited and annotated by
Rita Soulahian Kuyumjian

GOMIDAS
INSTITUTE

TEKEYAN
CULTURAL
ASSOCIATION

Trilogy - April 24, 1915

Aram Andonian, *Exile, Trauma and Death: On the Road to Chankiri with Komitas Vartabed,* transl, ed. and annot. by Rita Soulahian Kuyumjian.

Rita Soulahian Kuyumjian, *Teotig: Biography* with a translation by Ara Stepan Melkonian.

Rita Soulahian Kuyumjian, *The Survivor: Biography of Aram Andonian.*

Cover art by Anaït Abramian.

A joint publication of the Gomidas Institute and Tekeyan Cultural Association.

Printed by Taderon Press, 42 Blythe Rd., London W14 0HA, UK.

ISBN 978-1-903656-92-1

For more information please contact:
Gomidas Institute,
42 Blythe Rd.
London, W14 0HA, England.

Email: *info@gomidas.org*
Web: *www.gomidas.org*

*Dedicated to the Memory of Baidsar Nipiossian Bedevian,
beloved mother, grandmother and great-grandmother, who survived
the Deportations of Konia, Turkey in 1915*

Sarkis and Ruth Bedevian, New Jersey, USA

"The struggle of man against power is the struggle of memory against forgetting."

—Milan Kundera

CONTENTS

Acknowledgments

I would like to extend my gratitude to the following individuals and organizations for their help and advice in bringing this publication to light.

To the late Nourhan Ouzounian and Armine Keoshkerian of Montreal for encouraging me to translate Aram Andonian's articles to English. To Gourgen Gasparyan, of Charents Museum of Literature and Arts in Yerevan for preparing the pictures for volume one.

To Hilmar Kaiser, for his continuous encouragement through the translation of the works and advice on publishing them as a Trilogy.

To collaborators working on Trilogy-April 24, 1915. Ara Stephan Melkonian for his work on volume two. The latter could not be published without his valuable input. To a friend of the Armenian people, Victoria Hobson, for her editorial works on volume three. To Taline Sahakian Kuyumjian for her invaluable editorial input. To Aris Sevag for permission to use his translation of Aram Andonian's article "Pan Chega" for volume three.

To Raymond Kevorkian, historian and curator for AGBU Nubarian Library in Paris, who facilitated my research and gave me his insights on the first curator of Nubarian library, Aram Andonian. To Nazaret Salbashian of New York for his helpful suggestions during my research.

To supporters of the three volumes, Ruth and Sarkis Bedevian of New Jersey, the Kuyumjian family's grandchildren, Barkev Demirjian, Aline Koundakdjian, Araxi Ashadjian and Arman Kuyumjian, and the Tekeyan Cultural Association. They all believed in the merit of the work and gave their financial support.

Special thanks to Tekeyan Cultural Association for embracing this work as a joint publication between TCA and the Gomidas Institute.

To Der Vazken Kahana Boyadjian, Krikor Keusseyan, Vatche Ghazarian as well as the Tekeyan Cultural Association Montreal chapter, Hamazkayin Cultural Association of Montreal for lending me books and helping me with my research.

I would like to thank my husband and best friend Jirair, my son Arman and daughter in law Taline for their steadfast support and help for the publication of this work at its different stages.

My biggest thanks goes to the Gomidas Institute and Ara Sarafian for publishing the Trilogy, as well as the Institute's other projects related to modern Armenian history.

Rita Soulahian Kuyumjian, Montreal, Quebec

Foreword from TCA

Almost a century after the Armenian Genocide, and three generations later, from time to time new material seems to emerge to the light of day from evidences buried under the dust of decades, especially for the English language readership, to help keep the candle of our collective memory alight.

Dr. Rita Kuyumjian, a Montreal based professor of Psychiatry with a keen interest in Armenian art and history, embarked upon an extensive research more than a decade ago to study the medical aspect of Komitas Vartabed's mental derangement following his arrest and his ordeals in exile, where he witnessed the brutal murder of Armenian intellectuals near the remote village of Chankiri. Dr. Kuyumjian's search took her to the Villejuif Psychiatric Hospital in Paris, where the father of Armenian classic music and folk songs was treated after he survived the Genocide but never regained his sanity for the rest of his life. Dr. Kuyumjian then traced back the life of the great musical pioneer to Vienna, Istanbul, Yerevan, and Beirut, to put the pieces of the puzzle together with the help of historians and archival material stored in libraries. The results were crystallized in the book *Archeology of Madness: Komitas, Portrait of an Armenian Icon*, published in 2001 by the Gomidas Institute.

This exhaustive research revealed also a trove of documents by two other Constantinople Armenian intellectuals who narrowly escaped the Genocide: Teotoros Labjinjian (better known as Teotig) and Aram Andonian, both erudite writers and historians, who survived the Genocide and recorded not only their own arrests, exiles and ordeals, but also those of hundreds of other Armenian leaders and clergy, the cream of the crop of the Armenian community of the Ottoman Empire. The most poignant descriptions by Aram Andonian of Komitas' last few days before he was rescued, and of other intellectuals' before they were murdered have almost gone to oblivion, as well as Teotig's most comprehensive analysis of victimized Armenian leaders and clerics throughout the Ottoman Empire. These have now been translated from the original Armenian into English and supplemented by pertinent annotations and biographies by Dr. Rita Kuyumjian. These two almost forgotten scholars are resurrected by the current Trilogy-April 24, 1915 so that our English language readers become familiarized with the legacy of these two unsung heroes.

The Tekeyan Cultural Association (TCA) of the United States and Canada, true to its mission of sustaining and promoting the Armenian identity and culture in its broadest sense, is proud to participate in the joint efforts of the author, Dr. Rita Kuyumjian, the other co-sponsors Mr. and Mrs. Sarkis and Ruth Bedevian, the grandchildren of the Kuyumjian family, and of course the Gomidas Institute in London, England.

TCA - US and Canada

Introduction to Trilogy - April 24, 1915

The arrests of Constantinople Armenian intellectuals on April 24, 1915 marked the beginning of the Armenian Genocide. The first Genocide Memorial commemoration was organized four years later in April 1919 in Constantinople. The intellectuals who had survived the calamity wanted to pay homage and respect to the memory of those who were killed.

For the past 95 years, on April 24th, thousands of Armenians throughout the world, remember with reverence those who perished. My own family lost many members during this period.

However, the idea behind the publication of Trilogy - April 24 is to emphasize the importance of Constantinople intellectuals who survived this period and went on to record their personal narratives. These intellectuals went on to research, collect and publish the accounts of those who did not survive to tell their own stories. Two outstanding examples of such dedicated intellectuals are featured in the following three volumes. They are the historian-journalist Aram Andonian, and the publisher of the famous yearbooks *Amenouyn Daretsouytse* (Everyone's Almanac), Teotig.

Let me relate the story of the path of Trilogy - April 24, 1915 and its publication.

A decade ago, when I was researching Armenian Genocide literature for my work on Komitas' biography,[*] I found 25 fascinating articles published in an Armenian weekly in Paris. The weekly had a limited circulation and the articles had been forgotten. There was no doubt that I had discovered a first person account of the story of the first 72 hours of the Armenian Genocide, minute by minute, as it had unfolded. It was a story which was told with integrity, humor and dignity. That account needed to be told, this time to a wider audience, outside of the confines of Armenian readers. It had to be translated and published in English.

The first value of the book rested in the hundreds of names that were mentioned in the articles. They were the names of Armenian intellectuals of Constantinople who had been arrested. Although the names of the

[*] Rita Soulahian Kuyumjian, *Archeology of Madness: Komitas, Portrait of an Armenian Icon.* (Princeton and London: Gomidas Institute), 2001.

more prominent victims were familiar, many of the other names were little known. The passage of ninety years (and counting) was threatening to erase the identity of many of those noble men. Therefore, the names mentioned in the articles begged annotation. After all, those were the names of people who had been seen by the Young Turk dictators as the enemy of the state and were consequently jailed, exiled and brutally murdered. These victims were the intellectuals and leaders of the Armenian people who had dared to dream of equality and fraternity for their own people alongside the other ethnic and religious groups making up the Ottoman Empire.

My search for their biographies led me to the second person featured in Trilogy -April 24, 1915, Teotig and his *Houshartsan Nahadag Mdavoraganoutyan* (Monument to the Martyred Intellectuals). Teotig was well known for his yearbooks, *Amenoun Daretsouytsu* (Everyone's Almanac). One of his less well known works was on the martyred intellectuals of 1915. This book not only helped me annotate the 25 articles, but itself begged for the light of day with a translation into English.

Then my curiosity to know about Aram Andonian and Teotig led me to search for their biographies. I was interested to develop an understanding of the so-called "Bolsetsi mdavoragan", (the Constantinople Armenian intellectual) who had succeeded to promote western Armenian language and literature to new heights, to import a civil society movement into Constantinople, and to educate the Armenians deeply entrenched in the darkness of the Middle-Ages. Not finding their biographies, I was forced to write them myself.

Therefore the trilogy encompasses the works of the survivors Andonian and Teotig, their memories, recollections and testimonies, and the results of their research and publications.

The three volumes can be summaries as follows:

Trilogy - April 24, 1915. Volume One
Exile, Trauma and Death: On the Road to Chankiri with Komitas Vartabed
This first volume of Trilogy - April 24, 1915 is a translation of 25 articles written by Aram Andonian in Armenian. Andonian was commissioned to write them by the publishers of *Arevmoudk* for their special edition dedicated to Komitas Vartabed's 75th birthday. These articles were published in *Arevmoudk* during a seven month period from December 1946 to June 1947. The articles were called *"Komitasi hed. Inch*

baymannerou dag aratchatsav Komitasi mdki daknabu" (With Komitas: the circumstances which precipitated his mental turmoil). As the title implied, it was intended to highlight the Armenian composer's tragedy after his arrest and during his journey to exile. But the articles had unclogged the suppressed memory of those years in the author and the few articles that had been planned turned into a series that went beyond their initial mandate and covered the circumstances of not only Komitas' fate, but also the fate of all those intellectuals who were arrested during that same fateful night. Therefore, the initial title did not reflect the content of the series anymore. Each article was finished with the phrase "to be continued." The 25th article, despite the same ending, "to be continued", was to be the last installment. They left the reader suspended in air and wanting closure.

To transform the articles to a book required some additions and editorial intervention. A new title had to be adopted to reflect the content of the final work. The chapters were also given titles instead of numbers. The book also included a short epilogue. The annotations were used to give the reader an appreciation for the names mentioned in the articles. The pictures of the individuals mentioned added a welcome visual dimension to the verse. Everything else, including the unequal length of the chapters, were left as they were in the original series.

Trilogy - April 24, 1915. Volume Two

Teotig: Biography

with **"A Monument to the Martyred Intellectuals** (*Houshartsan Nahadag Mdavoraganoutyan*)**"** and **"A Literary Addition to the Monument, in Collaboration with the Survivors of the Armenian Genocide."**

This second volume of the trilogy has three parts. It starts with Teotig's biography with photographs from his well known almanacs.

The second part of the volume is a translation from Armenian to English of Teotig's work, *Houshartsan Abril 11.* (Monument to April 11). Teotig called it a "paper monument,"[*] the only monument to the Genocide in Constantinople,[†] hence the unusual title. The work was first published in Armenian in April 1919 on the occasion of the first organized memorial service in Constantinople dedicated to the Armenian Genocide.

---

[*]   Teotig, *Golgotha*, Introduction, p. 21. Antelias, Lebanon, 1966.
[†]   A Genocide monument was build in Istanbul but was confiscated by the Kemalists when they came to power. Now it is kept in one of the government buildings in Istanbul according to Turkish historian Ragip Zarakolu.

The April 11 Memorial Committee oversaw the publication as well as the memorial service. The proceeds of the publication were to form a Memorial Fund for the widows and orphans of the victims of April 24.

The date April 11 on the title sheet of the first publication of the book is based on the old Julian calendar used by Armenians, which is 13 days earlier than the Gregorian calendar. The old calendar is not in use any longer and April 11th is known as April 24th.

This work was reprinted several times. The first reprinting was done in 1939 in Alexandria, Egypt, during which it was revised, corrected and the name was changed to *Houshartsan Nahadag Mdavoraganoutyan* (Monument to the Martyred Intellectuals).[*] The second time it was reprinted was in Beirut, 1985. The present volume has been translated from a facsimile of the 1985 edition printed in Armenia in 1990 by the Central Bureau of the Communist Party of Armenia. This is the fourth edition of the work but the first one in English translation.[†]

The Monument contains the names and biographies of 763 Armenian leaders, writers, poets, doctors, lawyers, pharmacists, publishers, editors, deputies and members of the clergy (male and female, Apostolic, Catholic and Protestant Armenians), who perished during the Genocide. They are sub-categorized under the following sub-headings. Part 1, intellectuals, workers in the national-educational field, businessmen, those who died in exile of illness, those who were hanged in Constantinople. Part 2 lists the names of the martyrs by geographical district, and part 3 lists the names of the clergy. I added the name, picture and short biography of my own Kuyumjian family's great grand father, the musician and author of a book on khaz notation, the priest of Sourp Stepanos church in the village of Germir, near Caesarea [Kayseri], Der Stepan Kahana Kuyumjian.[‡]

The third part of volume two is a literary section that includes other survivor accounts from Chankiri and Ayash.[**]

---

[*]   Mher Garabedian, *Hayots 1915-1916 tvaganneri tseghasbannoutyan hartseru hay badmakroutyan mech* (The issue of the 1915-1916 Genocide in Armenian historiography) (Yerevan: Republic of Armenia, Academy of Sciences Publication), 1998, p. 111.

[†]   "The Monument to April 11" is being translated to Turkish as this publication goes to print.

[‡]   Teotig, *Golgotha*, (New York: St. Vartan Press), 1985.

[**] Ayash is the location where members of the Armenian political parties were exiled.

Trilogy - April 24, 1915. Volume Three

The Survivor: Biography of Aram Andonian

The third volume starts with a biography of the survivor Aram Andonian. A journalist by profession, Andonian documented the Genocide and published two important books immediately after the Mudros Armistice in 1918. *Medz Vodjiru* (The Great Crime) and *Ayn Sev Oreroun* (In Those Dark Days). He then became the first curator of the Nubarian Library of the Armenian General Benevolent Union in Paris. This library is an important depository related to 20th century Armenian history with its books and archives.

Part two of this volume is a literary addition, a translation by Aris Sevag of an article, "There is Nothing" by Aram Andonian, first published in his book, "In Those Dark Days."

Rita Soulahian Kuyumjian
February 11, 2010
Montreal, Quebec, Canada

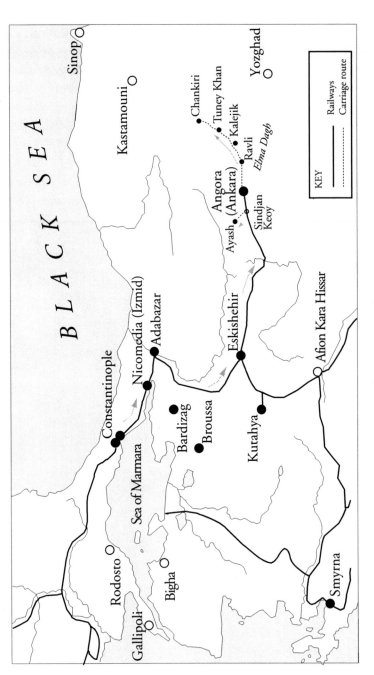

The Route to Exile

Exile
Trauma
and
Death

On the road to Chankiri with Komitas Vartabed

Chapter 1

The Courteous Arrests

It was only thirty-one years ago, when states and nations were engaged in mutual slaughter and the world was caught in a ghastly predicament, that our perplexed Armenian nation found itself alone and facing a group of murderers who had seized the leadership of Turkey and were destroying Armenians on their millennial homeland.

When these murderers had come to power, there was a major question that still needed resolution: the Armenian Question.[1] This matter received contradictory interpretations among different people and in different countries. However, in essence, it was nothing more than the desperate plea of a peaceful, hardworking and dynamic nation to be allowed to live free of oppression, vexation and arbitrary violence, and to eat its piece of bread, earned by the sweat of its brow, in peace.

The murderers I have alluded to used the conditions created by World War I to conceive their hellish scheme of eliminating the entire Armenian population of Turkey. Once and for all, they wanted to squash the legitimate and sacred right of Armenians to live in their own country. The presence of Armenians upset these Turks and thwarted their future plans and pretensions. They entrusted the realization of this plan to their most competent and capable leader, Talaat Pasha,[2] who was the Minister of Internal Affairs.

However, Talaat, despite being endowed with many abilities and a firmness of mind, never had the luck of completing any undertaking. His wife, Bayan Hayrie, on the occasion of the return of her husband's remains to Istanbul [1943], related to Hüseyin Cahid Yalçin that during the previous war, Wilhelm II had sent his personal painter to Constantinople to paint the portraits of Sultan Reshad, as well as those of Talaat, Enver[3] and Djemal Pashas.[4] However, Talaat's portrait remained unfinished. Bayan Hayrie added, "The poor pasha's destiny was predetermined. All his works remained unfinished. He did not witness the liberation of his country. He was halfway through when he was assassinated in a cowardly manner."[5]

We could forgive Bayan Hayrie for labeling Talaat's assassination "cowardly," but that would not be a proper description. Tehlirian,[6] who followed Talaat on Hardenberg Strasse in Charlottenburg, could have shot Talaat in the back, but he chose to pull the trigger while facing him, after he had called out his name. Talaat was wounded in his eye when he fell. It was Talaat who was the coward, as he had stabbed the Armenian people in the back, by duplicity and treachery, always with a smile on his lips and deception in his words. He did not even hesitate to send his friends of rainy days, friends who had collaborated with

Komitas Vartabed

him, to their death, with a "brotherly" smile, and murder in his mind.

Let's forgive Bayan Hayrie but complete her definition. Yes, Talaat gave a crushing blow to the Armenian people. At times and in many circumstances he was able to surpass history's most bloodthirsty criminals, but he was destined to fail in his plan to annihilate an entire nation. The proof is in today's Armenian diaspora and certainly in modern Yerevan; but the most timely and pertinent proof was his assassination.

Tehlirian's gesture, his desire to pull the trigger only after coming face to face with Talaat, was not an act of pointless vaunting. Talaat, himself a real wrestler with enormous physical force, could have, if he had the chance, destroyed the assassin's frail body with one punch.

"I simply wanted him to know that the blow was from an Armenian," said Tehlirian during that unforgettable day in Potsdam, on June 6, 1921, while enjoying the hospitality of Dr. Lepsius[7] in his house.

As it is known, the first phase of the implementation of the plan conceived by Talaat and the Ittihadist conspirators was the arrest of Armenian intellectuals of Constantinople, on the eve of Saturday April 24th, 1915.[8] We were the first to be arrested and Komitas Vartabed[9] was among us. We were more than 200 people in the central jail of

Constantinople and very few of us survived either by luck or by various chance happenings. The others were killed under horrendous conditions, in groups or individually, often miles away from each other. The survivors did not escape unscathed from this ordeal and each of them, as in the case of the ill-fated Komitas Vartabed, forever bore the consequences of the devilish actions of Talaat and his collaborators.

On the occasion of Komitas' 75th birthday commemoration, I take the liberty to put on paper some memories of that tragic night, and the ominous days that followed. These memories do not pretend to draw a comprehensive picture of that horrendous genocide. To describe it fully, one would need to fill volumes. My goal is to describe the tragic fate that befell Komitas, also the events and circumstances that led to the disturbance of his brilliant and god-bestowed intellect, which in itself was music, a melody in whatever mode it was played.

Some diversions from the main text and certain details that the reader may encounter serve no other purpose but to portray the various psychological states that we experienced, personally or as a group, at the beginning of those horrible events.

On the 24th of April, 1915, that Saturday night, Komitas was one of the first arrested. The Pangalti neighborhood where Komitas lived was swarming with spies and informers. It is superfluous to state that among them were also Armenians, more than Turks.

Seven years earlier, during the early days of the reestablishment of the Constitution, the Ittihadist gangs filled garbage carts with these rogues and paraded them on the streets of Constantinople so people could spit at them and shower them with unspeakable obscenities as a reward for their exploits. The same Ittihadists, soon after taking the reigns of government, duly recalled to duty all those spies, whose numbers swelled every day with groups of newcomers.[10]

The majority of the spies were doing their work in the vicinity of Pera. Almost all of us had been under their surveillance for months, without feeling or, more correctly, without paying much attention to it, because the fall of the capital [to the Allied Powers] seemed imminent during that tragic month of April 1915. It was no secret that the government was moving from Constantinople to Konia, which was going to serve as a temporary capital of Turkey. Many people had become aware that two special trains were ready waiting at Haydar Pasha station, one to transport the political corps and the other the sultan and his followers. The last train was also to carry ministers and senior government officials. That train was also designated to transport Patriarch Zaven,[11] the Greek Patriarch, as well the Chief Rabbi who were officially notified to be ready to leave at once on short notice. Many Turks were sending their families to the province. The banks, by government order, were transporting their gold bullion reserves to cities in the interior where they had branches. A large majority of Constantinople residents believed that the allied forces were going to celebrate their Easter mass in Aya Sophia mosque.[12] Therefore, who was paying attention to spies?

The spies who worked around the Pangalti neighborhood were aware of Komitas' routine of returning home early. They arrested him without a long wait or caution, unlike what they were obliged to do with many of us who spent most of the evenings outside due to many engagements. We also had different habits in comparison to the doomed Vartabed, who did not cause them any grief.

The arrest of Komitas, like many of the other arrests that night, did not attract attention and we did not know how it took place. When I went home – our home was a few steps away from his – my family was not aware of any developments. Later on, when we realized that the general circumstances were the same for all of us, we did not inquire further into Komitas' arrest. In reality, it was not even an arrest, as it was an invitation by a plain clothed police officer, smiling and courteous, asking us to accompany him to the neighborhood police station, where the Commissar Bey, as they were called, wanted to ask us for a little information. "It won't take more than five minutes, you will soon be back, nothing of importance..."

This was the general watchword.

Do not forget that I am alluding to the first wave of arrests on April 24th in Constantinople. In the provinces or the later arrests in Constantinople could have been under completely different conditions. But our arrests took place with great tact. And this was not surprising. For it was an essential condition for the success of the criminal government's plans to show utmost tactfulness. They had cast their net wide, and they had to exercise extreme caution to ensure a big catch at once. For this reason, it was important not to make noise, to avoid resistance, to avoid incidents, to avoid publicity, to avoid people going underground, and to decrease the number of those who, by various means, might escape from the hell of Turkey.

There were a few exceptions when, instead of the enchanting tune of the piper leading us to the police station, there was actual police brutality. Some policemen had not been able to understand the given watchword and yielded to their innate sense of cruelty. But the majority of the police force, which was chosen to carry out this task, excelled in carrying out their orders. In a few cases they inspired such confidence that the arrested, who were reclining in their pajamas on their sofas, truly believed that they would be back in a few minutes and came to the police station without changing their clothes. They were in

Patriarch Zaven Der Yeghiayan

their night attire or light indoor wear, without socks or slippers. Poor things, they were driven to their destinations, Ayash or Chankiri, in those clothes. And the weather was cold.

At the police station in Pangalti, where they took me, there were already a few "guests" who had arrived before me. Among them were Sarkis Minasian,[13] Gigo,[14] Khachig Idaredjian, Dr. Allaverdi,[15] and others whom I did not recognize. After I arrived, new groups continued to arrive and soon we were numbered more than twenty. The rooms that were allocated to us were on the first floor, where we were rushed after being subjected to detailed searches. We were ordered from the ground floor not to speak to each other. But there was only one Turkish gendarme assigned to guard us, and we soon familiarized ourselves with him. When we had something to tell each other – and we had so many questions to ask – we would address the gendarme in Armenian, while offering him a cigarette. Of course the man did not understand what he was told, but he might have thought that we were exchanging courtesies and took the cigarette with a smile.

And the one to whom the words were actually addressed responded in the kind offering of another cigarette to the man. This game went on for a while until the gendarme was tired of the words directed at him and, having amassed a significant stock of cigarettes, went into a corner and started to smoke, leaving us free to talk to each other as we wished.

Few of us, including myself, believed that these arrests were leading to exile. But we were not really sure, because the composition of the group was not uniform. There were people in the group whom we saw for the first time and it was difficult to imagine that they could have played any role in national or governmental affairs. For instance, the Armenian butcher on our street, Agha Garabed, was fooled by the words of the gendarme and came to the police station without feeling the need to even take off his bloodstained and smelly apron. The steel knife-sharpener was still fastened to his belt. And that is how he found himself in Ayash, the destination of his exile. He did not even close his shop and left the day's earning in the drawer. The poor soul could not fathom what his relationship was to people "like us." It was not even obvious what "like us" meant in his mind and, in any way, he was right.

Later we were also going to see among us a man named Asadourian Artin, a surprising person whose identity was perhaps mistaken, and he was arrested instead of someone else. Similar mishaps were plenty that night. This Asadourian fellow was a penniless and really harmless man. He neither knew how to read nor write. He had no profession and for some time he was the municipality's dog catcher on the streets of Constantinople. It should not be forgotten, of course, that the Ittihadists first tested their massive exile plan on the dogs of Constantinople – and I am alluding to the four legged creatures. They killed the defiant and biting ones on the spot and banished the remaining ones to one of the Princes Islands, where most of them perished of hunger or tore each other to pieces. Their screeches reached Constantinople when the wind blew in the city's direction.

What was this poor dog collector doing among us? We could not stop our giggles when he went on muttering, "The work was *parlakh* [wonderful]. When the dogs were plenty in the city, for each dog they paid me 40 para. Now that the dogs are scarce and I have to look for them even harder, they pay me no more than three ghurush. *Hey vakh...*"

Among us there were even Ittihadist Armenians. Let me mention just one, Dr. Dikran Allahverdi. The latter was the director of the Pangalti branch of the most powerful organization that the Ittihadists created, the *Mudaafat Milli* [National Defense Council], which Armenians feared the most. This "blessed" person was not a "passive" Ittihadist, but a highly active member of the party, who had just raised 3,000 Ottoman gold liras, which at the time, deservedly, gained him the accolade of the Turkish papers. 3,000 gold liras was not a small sum at a time when Ottoman paper currency held its value.

Shavarsh Missakian

He was also fooled and brought to the police station in the same manner as the others. Even after his arrival he could not fathom what was going on. After a while he dared to ask the guard to pass a message to the Commissar, that his bed-time had passed, and that he wanted the Commissar Bey to call him and tell him what he had to say and let him go home to sleep.

The gendarme did not pay any attention and did not even budge from his seat. But I remember our roar and laughter that was triggered by the words of this innocent man, "The doctor's bedtime has passed."

"Doctor, we will catch our first sleep in Konya," yelled Gigo from his corner.

The man did not even have time to understand better, because at that time a group of secret police agents came to our floor. They were always Armenians accompanied by Turkish agents. They made us descend to the ground floor and hurled us into newly bought red fire trucks from Europe. They sat a secret police agent beside each one of us. The reason for this excessive caution was the fear that we might make noise and attract the attention of passers-by, thus alerting those who were not arrested yet to leave their residences.

On the street other trucks similar to ours were lined up against the wall of the guard-house. It was obvious that others had been transported somewhere else and would follow us. Komitas was surely among the first to be taken there, but we did not think of him at the time, because we had no idea of the extent of the arrests and could not suppose that clergymen would be sharing our luck as well.

Zabel Yesayan

The truck we were stuffed into more or less, after long and winded detours, took us to the central jail of Constantinople where Ibrahim Effendi[16] greeted us. I have not forgotten that this blood stained man became infamous for his genocidal crimes in Bithynia.[17] It was on his orders that poor Ardashes Haroutiunian[18] and his father, after long days of horrendous tortures, were martyred. That night he received us with forced but impeccable courtesy. The word of the day was the same everywhere. Later he murmured a few things, not greetings of welcome of course, but neither words of reprimand. Without further delay he led us to the office of the political section of the jail, where Reshad Bey[19] was waiting for us in a long and narrow hall, behind a table covered with huge folders, with a satanic and sarcastic smile on his face. There were two lists on the table, which Reshad Bey started to read, instructing us to say *mevjud* [present] when our name was called. Every time one of us pronounced that word, Reshad Bey would mark the list with a pencil.

This was the extent of the entire interrogation in that odd calamity which would have such a tragic ending.

Reshad Bey did not read every name. But whatever he read was informative for us. We did not know who was brought in before us, but we now knew who else would be brought in after us.

Many people were coming to join us in jail that same night or the day after. Others, who were able to escape that night, were arrested after a while and exiled either alone or in small groups. And some of them, like Chifte-Saraf, Sirouni,[20] and others were able to remain in Constantinople, forgotten or in permanent hiding. Alexander Panosian was to be arrested and soon released. Few people, among them Hagop Oshagan[21] and Zabel Yesayan,[22] were able to flee to Bulgaria. Shavarsh Misakian,[23] on the other hand, while attempting the same escape route, was captured and spent the entire duration of the war in jail under truly atrocious conditions.

After reading his list of names, Reshad Bey put the two lists on the table and called the director of the jail, Ibrahim Effendi, without addressing us. It was a short and curt order, "Take the Effendis to the *misafirhane* [guest house]."

One did not have to be a genius to understand that by *misafirhane* he referred to jail. Was the use of the term simple sarcasm or a word of consideration? It is difficult to comprehend the Turkish mind when it uses courtesy to veil its true thoughts. On the other hand, in natural rudeness, yelling, swearing, slandering and abusiveness – much less dangerous than the latter courtesy – it is like an open book, easy to read and easy to grasp.

Chapter 2

A Comedy or a Death Sentence?

Passing many doors with multiple locks and keys, an absolute labyrinth of iron trellises, we entered the large square of Mehterhane prison. Two rooms were allocated for the "guests" of the day. First was the awe-inspiring principal building of the jail, located on our right side. Facing us on the other end of the square was the Subyan Mektebi, the section for juvenile criminals. In that section there was a school hall as well. The jail was famous for clandestine, sexual and inhuman abuses. The rich and famous, for whom money was not an issue, had access to it. Both the jail and the juvenile correctional "school" had been vacated of their usual inmates three days earlier and transferred to other jails. They had cleaned the buildings and the floors were still partially wet.

None of us were able to enter Subyan Mektebi because it was already full when we arrived and its doors were shut closed. Since this jail was allocated to the "famous" detainees, a few of the later arrivals, such as Diran Kelegian,[24] Dr. Stephan Miskdjian,[25] his brother the pharmacist Krikor Miskdjian, Dr. Bazil Khan and others were placed in one of the rooms used by the administration. But soon that room was also full to capacity. Having no choice, the new arrivals were now directed, without any distinction, to the main hall on the first floor of the principal building of the jail, the *govoush*, which was assigned to "common" people.

They allowed one exception in our group. They separated Dr. Allahverdi and put him with the lucky group in the administration building. We were taken directly to the govoush. There weren't any cells in that hall. The cells, usually assigned to dangerous criminals, were located in the basement and remained closed to us. It is unbelievable how many surprising encounters we had in that hall, despite the fact that those gathered were only a small fraction of the arrested. Everybody knew about others who were taken to other detention centers and we soon had a general idea about the whole affair. The vast majority of [Armenian] intellectuals of Constantinople were now in jail: writers, journalists, doctors, dentists, pharmacists, actors, lawyers, architects, followers of fine arts, national and government employees, attachés of foreign consulates, members of the Ottoman parliament and [Armenian] National Committees, businessmen, school principles, teachers, students, and tradesmen. In addition there were other groups whose identity and social status were not known to us and we were clueless who they were. Trapped and brought over were the true gang leaders, the Kulhan Beys, and famous *ayingadjis* [tobacco traffickers] from Kum Kapou, Gedig Pasha and Samatia, who had not only terrorized peaceful people but members of the police force as well. They felt at home in that govoush, as they were familiar with the place and jail guards, and they occupied the best spots. One of them yelled out loud as a response to the ones who forebode the future.

"I have been here five times… do not worry, we will come out of here… one can only not escape from the graveyard."

Soon we became aware that among the arrested were also members of the clergy. We were told the name of Komitas Vartabed. In fact, he was brought to jail early on and was led to Subyan Mektebi.

Later on we found out that the first person who knew about his arrest was his neighbor, Dr. Avedis Nakkashian, although not on the same night but the next morning. Komitas had a servant from Van, Varbed Garabed, who waited for his master's return all night. Early morning, realizing that Komitas had not returned, he rushed to the residence of Dr. Nakkashian, almost short of breath, visibly upset, unable to utter a word for a minute.

The doctor thought that Komitas must have had some sudden distress and started to put on his clothes in a hurry.

Finally Garabed collected himself and said in a tragic tone

"They took him doctor, they took him…"

"What did they take?"

"They took the reverend father."

"But who took him?"

"The police took him during the night."

Dr. Nakkashian, to whom the arrest of the vartabed did not sound plausible, prepared to leave the house in order to go to the corner guard house and to look for Komitas. However, he had no time, because soon afterwards, he too was arrested.

We were also informed about the names of other clergymen, Hovnan Vartabed Garabedian, Rev. Der Vartan from Ferikiugh (Ferikeoy), Rev. Father Housig Kachouni and Father Krikoris Balakian.[26] The last one was arrested for a completely different reason, based on the complaint of Patriarch Zaven who had accused Balakian of endangering the political standing of the Church Council in its relations with the Ottoman government. I do not know the details, nor the truth behind this accusation. It is a dark story and probably Zaven Srpazan will shed light on it in his memoirs, which he is writing at the moment in Beirut.[27]

Mourad (Hampartsoum Boyadjian)

All these clergymen were in Subyan Mektebi. There were also the most prominent members of different political parties, alongside writers, various functionaries, and certain people of good social standing and competence.

What dumbfounded us most from the first moment was the fact that there was no obvious direction or trend in the arrests. With the revolutionaries were also anti-revolutionaries. There were even people the revolutionaries were not reluctant to call *sheriatjis*. There were liberals as well as conservatives. There were educated people with complete illiterates. There were the hot headed alongside the most cautious of people who were even scared of their own shadows. People who were in essence in opposite camps and even those who had fought each other were lumped together.

This attempt to mix water with fire worried us. Of course we did not know why we were arrested and what would be the outcome of this mishap. It was obvious that there was a serious and troublesome threat facing not only this or that faction of the Armenian people, but a threat that was looming over the whole nation. Our assembly in the ominous surroundings of the central jail was simply the symbol of a horrendous organized drama.

We saw Komitas the following Sunday morning when the doors of Subyan Mektebi opened and people came out. Soon, the lucky ones who spent the night in the administration rooms joined us. We sarcastically called their arrangements *mevkili* [first class], though according to their story, they spent the night as uncomfortably as we did in the second and third class rooms.

Dr. Stepan Miskdjian, who was a tall and very kind person, told us with laughter that the room was so narrow that after lying down he

Ardzrouni - Hakob-Avedisian

could not stretch his legs even half way.

At first, after we were gathered there, certain partisan groups were formed around us. Tashnagtsagans [members of the Armenian Revolutionary Federation] were side by side: Agnouni,[28] Khajag,[29] Siamanto,[30] Haroutiun Shahrigian,[31] Roupen Zartarian,[32] Hayg Tiryakian,[33] Sarkis Minasian, Marzbed,[34] Shavarsh Krisian,[35] Parsegh Shahbaz,[36] Melkon Gurdjian,[37] Dr. Armenag Parseghian, Taniel Varoujan,[38] Aris Israyelian,[39] Dr. Garabed Pashayan,[40] Hampartsoum Hampartsoumian,[41] Nerses Papazian,[42] Kegham Parseghian,[43] Sarkis Srents,[44] Partogh Zorian,[45] Dr. Mirza Ketendjian, Yenovk Shahen,[46] his brother, Krikor Ankout,[47] and Mihrtad Haygazn.[48] And still I do not name all of them.

Little further the Hunchagians Mourad,[49] Dr. Krikor Djelal,[50] Ardzrouni,[51] Stepan Tanielian, Hagop Terzian,[52] Samvel Toumajan, Hovhaness Keledjian, Haroutiun Djangulian[53] and others who were gathered around their elder man Sako.[54]

With us were the non-party members Dr. Daghavarian,[55] Dr. K. Boghosian,[56] Krikor Torosian (Gigo), Mikayel Shamdandjian,[57] Piuzant Bozadjian,[58] Vramshabuh Samveloff,[59] pharmacist Hagop Nargiledjian[60] who had come in his uniform, the banker Terlemezian, Roupen Sevag,[61] Yervant Chavoushian, Abraham Hayrigian.

A separate group was formed by Diran Kelegian, Piuzant Kechian Dr. Hagop Topdjian, Kasbar Cheraz, Rev. Keropian,[62] Arisdages

Kasbarian, Hagop Gorian, architect Simon Melkonian, Krikor Ohnigian with his three sons, and a few businessmen.

But these groupings did not last very long. Soon people mingled. The conversations were centered around the circumstances of each person's arrest, on the "absent" ones, on the intention of the gangs heading the government, on the possibility of finding people to intervene on all our behalf – or at least some of us – as well as the continuing war. Among us, of course, there were those who were discouraged, confused, and uttered words of sorrow. But in general we heard jokes, witty remarks, even loud laughter, which soon dampened the black thoughts of the pessimists and prevented negative thoughts from spreading.

Krikor Ankut

There was noting unusual in the appearance of Komitas. He was joking in his usual manner, calling his acquaintances *kertenkele*s [lizards], which was, of course, a good sign. His fiery and sarcastic gaze screened those present and rested his eyes on familiar faces.

"You too are here *kertenkele…*" or "Couldn't you just hide under a stone and escape, *ha kertenkele!*"

Of course he had not spent a good night on the humid floors of Subyan Mektebi. But his usual bed was also a wooden plank, covered with a thin sheet. He did not like to sleep on a soft bed. He was annoyed a little during the night by the crowd of people, especially the cigarette smoke, which simply irritated him.

When he came close to us, he was not worried about himself. He did not express any words that would indicate inner distress. Like many others, he also hoped that this "joke" (he used this term) was not going to last long. The Patriarch and the Armenian National Council, through the influence of Armenian deputies in the Ottoman government, and the intervention of foreign consulates, would put an end to this calamity.

Consequently, because of this optimism, he was able to laugh off the pessimism and hopelessness of a few prominent individuals, which he witnessed during the night, specially Dr. Torkomian.

"He was crying," he said astonished, alluding to the doctor.

A little later, Dr. Torkomian,[63] who had joined us, confirmed that he had truly spent the entire night crying and the vartabed had really tried hard to console him.

"If it wasn't for his support I might have passed away," he uttered literally.

Then he added that these arrests were not going to lead to a benign ending and that he was going to be one of the first victims.

Nerses Papazian

The doctor's premonition was going to be correct… but in a different way. He was not going to be one of the first to be slaughtered, but among the first to survive.

Torkomian recounted the circumstances of his arrest, which was the same as what had happened to us. After midnight, they had escorted him to Tarlabashi guard house, where he met Arisdages Kasbarian,[64] Dr. Krikor Djelal and others. Some time later came Piuzant Kechian,[65] Serovpe Noradoungian,[66] Hampartsoum Hampartsoumian, Roupen Zartarian, Dr. Bazil Khan and Apig Djambaz.[67] They had been brought to jail in automobiles after being subjected to the same formalities, and then squeezed into Subyan Mektebi, where the doctor saw Komitas and stuck to him all night.

I give this particular detail in order to tell you about one of the doctor's friends of that night, Apig Djambaz, who was the only one among us who was going to be killed against the government's will.

Chapter 3

Rules at Mehterhane Prison

Apig Djambaz was a Turkophone Catholic Armenian who complained constantly that he was not Armenian, that he was Catholic, and that he was arrested by mistake. He complained in jail, on route to exile, on the steam boat, on the train and at the station. The man was old and despite his obsessive preoccupation with his Catholicism, he was a very pleasant joker. Therefore, we were not offended by his denial of his Armenian identity. As if to react to his denial, we insisted on calling him "Djambazian," which really irritated him.

"*Yok, yok,*" he yelled, "*Benim ismim Djambaz der, ben Djambazian deyil yim* [No, no, my name is Djambaz, I am not Djambazian]."

"*Hakenez var, Djambazian Effendi* [You are right Djambazian Effendi]" we said, always emphasizing the *"ian."*

He left with hasty steps, leaving the impression of being scared of losing control of his temper and giving into his desire to curse.

It was natural that the clerks, like us, did not give any consideration to his Catholicism.[68] There were other Catholics among us, as well as Protestants.[69] Djambaz was exiled to Chankiri with us. In Chankiri he did not stop complaining. He sent telegrams to Constantinople many times and presented petitions to Mutasaref Asaf Bey,[70] who was finally disturbed enough to get rid of this problem. Asaf Bey personally intervened at the Ministry of Interior in Constantinople and received permission for his release.

When the order arrived and was communicated to him, Djambaz screamed at us, "You see? Didn't I tell you that I am not Armenian? I am Catholic... now you stay and I leave!"

The "you stay" was not very Catholic but we were all happy that the old man was free.

The next day, he was able to hire a cart to Angora [Ankara] and then on to Constantinople. Many of us advised him not to leave alone but to wait for other lucky people like him who might be permitted to leave. For safety purposes they could leave as a group, under the supervision of the police. But he did not listen. It was his fate not to see Constantinople again. On the route between Tuney and Kalejik, the Kurdish Alo gangsters from Boyreg, who had infested that area, stopped the cart. Without paying attention to his screaming that he was not Armenian but Catholic and had permission from the Ministry of Interior to go to Constantinople, they simply shot and robbed him. Most probably the coach driver, who was hired in Chankiri – an Albanian by the name of Hasan, a criminal with a 15 year jail sentence – was himself part of the gang and had informed his culprits that Djambaz was carrying money on him, which was true. The recipient of the stolen goods was a Turk by the name of Edhem who was the lessee of Tuney Khan.

On August 12, 1915, at the instigation of Djemal Oghuz Bey (the Ittihadist responsible secretary for Chankiri), the same gang members of Kurd Alo killed, also in front of Tuney Khan, Taniel Varoujan and Roupen Chilingirian [Sevag], along with their three friends, the bookbinder Onnig Maghazajian,[71] the baker Artin Agha from Ortakiugh [Ortakeoy], and the blacksmith Vahan Kehya. (The latter had allocated his free time to building bombs, but that is a different story).

Because I have made this detour, let me also mention that under different circumstances, the fate that befell Apig Djambaz also befell another exiled friend, a member of the Armenian National Assembly, Arisdages Kasbarian. Because of a mistake, the telegram for his release arrived in Chankiri instead of Ayash where he was detained. Of course, we sent a telegram to Ayash without losing time so he could correct the mistake and take advantage of the freedom given him. But three days were lost by the time he received this news. Later, in Angora hospital, I learned that just one day before sending the telegram, Arisdages Kasbarian was killed... Had the order gone straight to Ayash, Kasbarian could have survived, because all of our friends who were released from Ayash returned to Constantinople safely.

Let us now return to our jail.

In the courtyard of Mehterhane prison the guards had given us complete freedom. Throughout the night they had given themselves to the business of renting pillows and blankets and left us alone. There was no surveillance over us. We were, in general, very calm guests, drastically different from their usual clients.

I have to confess that the hospitality of Turkish jails at that time could not be compared with the rest of the world. Inside jails national,

racial and religious discrimination disappeared. Every inmate was
equally guilty in the eyes of the authorities who had thrown people in
jail, lawfully or not, that was not an issue. Soon an understanding
would develop among the guards, especially if the newcomers had
money and were not stingy, and they would sometimes share some of
their pleasure with them. The strongest and most powerful occupied a
privileged position. The ones without means achieved the same ends
with flattery and lots of careful circumspect attention.

One could find everything in jail... things unimaginable.... The
guards pretended not to see for the sake of money or out of fear. In
jails, where there were inmates for 101 years – effectively people
sentenced to life in prison – the issue was simple. Such criminals were
already sentenced to maximum prison terms and had no fear of
additional sentences, so they could kill the guards. They, as well as
others, always had a dagger in their possession, despite very rigorous
searches. If they were caught, they would hand the daggers to the
guards and simply repossess them later.

During the four years of my exile, I was an inmate in more than 20
jails, to be precise 23, not counting different detention rooms and
stables which served as jails where there were none. Not counting the
famous Sidikli jail in Konia – which had its several "charms" such as its
delicious tea prepared by a Persian inmate – I left them quite
unwillingly. We had become nomads with no home to call our own,
destined to walk incessantly like the proverbial wandering Jew. The
road in front of us was long and led to the distant desert destined for
us. During the cruel journey, jails became rest areas and had some
advantages. Arak and cognac were not in short supply and were served
secretly in coffee cups, but they had to be gulped down at once without
any delay. I don't mention the hashish, of which no jail was deprived,
among the 23 that were part of my allotment.

The central jail, like the others, had its special coffee-maker. We
were told that after being an inmate for many years, this man had been
released but had not been able to live outside. Nostalgically, he went
back and knocked at the door of the jail. Of course the door remained
closed to him. Somebody advised him to commit a serious crime and
receive another sentence to be sent to jail again. But the man, having
aged, had lost his desire for new adventures. Finally, he was able to
convince the coffee maker at the jail to retire against some sum and he
occupied his place. Of course this man had never had so many orders

for coffee or tea before. He had never had such a big crowd in the jail before. He struck an agreement with the guards and raised the price from the usual 10 paras to 20 paras, and they constantly supplied us with tea, milk or coffee. During the night, when we were all cold, the hot tea felt like a blessing. Among us the Russian-Armenians and the Iranian-Armenians ordered four-five cups in a row.

The last two people who were arrested and brought to jail were Smpad Piurad[72] and Hayg Khodjasarian.[73] Poor Piurad, who had published a long series of complex novels exalting heroes [*herosabadoum*], left the impression that he was a brave man. However, he was so affected by his arrest that he could not utter a word for several minutes. It is also true that this state of mind did not last very long and he soon became most talkative. We found out from Khodjasarian and others that news of our arrests was widely circulated, fear was reigning everywhere, and one could not find a single Armenian soul on the streets.

My friends of Pera were eager to start a hand of Sixty-six but were unable to buy a deck of cards. It was probably strictly forbidden. They collected same size cardboard boxes of cigarettes and brought them to me. I was to draw the signs and pictures of the cards.

Despite the strict searches of the previous night, many were able to hide pencils, even color pencils, which made my little task easier. The signs were soon drawn. The pictures of the kings, queens and princes, which I was drawing on the backs of one or another detainee, were nothing but caricatures of a few of my prison mates. Those who were most scared, I pictured in female clothes and long hair, to create the quartet of the dames. Komitas was one of the kings, with a long beard and a few lizards attached to them, his unforgettable *kertenkelles*.

As soon as I drew these cartoons, they were passed from one hand to the other. Later it was difficult to collect them back and finish the deck. They did not serve any purpose anyway because the day's events would not allow for a game of cards. In the evening, the only time when four people gathered face to face to start a game, was the moment when the comedy, which we stubbornly insisted on believing in, was going to change and become a most awful tragedy.

At the time these cards were drawn, the majority who shared our luck were calm, each one busy with something, some giving themselves to more or less serious discussion, mainly about the probable fall of Constantinople. Meanwhile, the poor guards were broken into a sweat, running around trying to carry out an order to gather us in a certain corner of the square in front of a police officer surrounded by a few guards.

A tall, pale-faced, excessively thin young man with a long and sharp nose soon sprouted on top of a marble bench and prepared to read

Dr. Nazaret Daghavarian, founding member of the AGBU

our names from lists which he held in his hand. His task was to register the names of the lucky ones who had the fortune of enjoying the hospitality of the "hotel" which was going to destroy them.

Komitas was close to us, surrounded by unfamiliar people who were caught in a heated argument. We could not comprehend what the argument was about, but they were making noise, while the clerk, visibly annoyed, was waiting for silence to resume his reading.

"Shush," whispered Komitas, "Let the stork call…"

That clerk really had the looks of a stork perched on that bench.

We were once more instructed, as we had done once in front of Reshad Bey, to call *mevjud* [present], when our names were read.

And the stork started to call.

But soon another kind of noise was going to reign, the noise of our giggles. The clerk, who obviously was not very familiar with Armenian names, called out some of our names, and the names of absent ones, with such comical distortion, that it was impossible for us to remain serious. We all started to laugh.

The man remained unabashed. Before pronouncing each name, he waited, deliberated, and read in a hurried gasp, as he was scared that he would forget and be obliged to check it again. Of course, most of the time the names that he uttered were correct, or little distorted, but a few were subjected to ridiculous and unrecognizable transformations.

For example, Heygaz Mehurdar, Tiriyaki Hayik, Daghyeyen Nezaret, Miskin Doctor, Djihangirli Artin, Udi Yervant, and other similar names were subjected to stupendous transfigurations, which were followed by our tumult of giggles. It was some task to guess that those were the names of Mihrtad Haygazn, Hayg Tiryakian, Dr. Nazaret Daghavarian, Dr. Miskdjian, Haroutiun Djangulian, Yervant Odian.[74]

It was a free spectacle, to which we were becoming unwitting spectators, and it seemed funny at least at the outset.

After my name was called, I separated from the group to look for the cards that I had drawn and left in the possession of different people. Later I was told that Komitas also had his share of being renamed. The clerk, when it was Komitas' name, took time to sound it out, "Kom...Komi... Komita..." and then probably mixed the end "s" with the Arabic "j" and "ye" combined letters and yelled in a hurry, "Komita-Dji rahib..." which plainly meant "revolutionary priest."

It was said that Komitas was really shaken from this unexpected nomination, which of course was not welcome under the circumstances we found ourselves, and in his confusion he repeatedly answered, "*mevduj, mevduj*" instead of answering "*mevjud.*"

Even in that confusion, it could not have been that Komitas forgot how to speak Turkish, which was his mother tongue, as was the case with all Armenians living in the region of Gudina [Kutahya]. Komitas had only later learned Armenian in Etchmiadzin. Most probably he had intentionally reversed the letters of the word *mevjud* as a response to the distortion of his name. We knew that he liked to joke, and he joked on all occasions, sometimes in the most unexpected circumstances.

When this comedy ended, they started to distribute bread to us. Although we were hungry, the distribution of bread made us feel uncomfortable and left us with an uneasy feeling. Even those who had seen their friends and relatives and were surrounded by acquaintances; or others who had without any precaution — even with arrogance — the guts to talk, argue, and joke at some surprising moments; even those who had forgotten or did not want to think where they were, now had the same gut wrenching feeling: the distribution of bread brought home the reality that they were in jail, that they had lost their freedom, and that they were caught like mice in a trap. They knew that their circumstances in the political climate of those days could lead to tragic consequences.

Hunger also had a say as well, louder and more demanding than other worries and concerns. Everyone received their allocated portion. The bread that was distributed was black *tayij*, which many preferred over the white bread of Constantinople. It was still hot and we put it under our left arms and, bite by bite, started to chew. Mihrtad Haygazn, who was acquainted with life in prison, yelled, "The bread is for the whole day, keep some of it for the night."

Komitas also had his bread under his arm and was surrounded with sympathetic admirers who had succeeded in buying olives, cheese, dried figs, or boiled eggs from the

Ambassador Henry Morgenthau

grocery store in the jail. They were extending him their full palms, so he could have whatever he wished with his bread. But Komitas hardly reached out to those hands.

My friends of Pera finally succeeded in finishing the deck of cards, which I had started to draw. They were looking for a convenient corner to start their game of Sixty-six. The game called Sixty-six was as popular in Constantinople at that time as the game called Blot is in French society today. But our friends did not have time to decide in which corner to play the game because suddenly the guards announced that we were allowed to write letters to our families asking for change of clothes, bedding, money and food.

Of course this announcement was not auspicious news, simply a revelation that our confinement could last a while, but perhaps nobody wanted to reflect on that thought. Then the guards announced that the letters had to be written on postcards and only in Turkish. We were also permitted to telegraph. We bought the cards from them, and of course they took great advantage of this God given opportunity. They even returned, for pay, the pencils they had confiscated from us the night of our arrest during their searches.

Nobody paid attention to these details. Everyone was in a rush to take advantage of the opportunity without delay. But many, who could not write one word of Turkish, were confused and wondered around with their cards, looking for help. Their difficulty was soon noticed and self-assigned volunteer-secretaries appeared. These were Sarkis Srents, Abraham Hayrigian, Dr. Avedis Nakkashian,[75] who had just arrived after the bread distribution, Yervant Chavoushian, Kasbar Cheraz, Kegham Parseghian, Arisdages Kasbarian, Piuzant Kechian, and with them a few city officials who, after writing their personal letters, offered their knowledge of Turkish to the needy and finished their tasks. A few people, like Piuzant Kechian, Dr. Torkomian, Jacques Sayabalian,[76] preferred to send telegrams.

I do not know to whom Komitas turned for help. Although he knew Turkish, he could not write it. Yenovk Shahen, who had brought the written cards to the secretarial office of the jail, told us that he had received two cards from Komitas, one addressed to his home address, surely to Garabed Varbed, and the other to the translator who worked at the American Embassy, Mr. Arshag Schmavonian.[77] Komitas was well known at the American Embassy, where he was very much loved. Mrs. Morgenthau often invited him to perform at gatherings at the embassy, where he sang and played for the guests during evening receptions. Even on March 4th 1914, he had organized a small concert in the halls of the embassy with 24 singers, mixed male and female, from his "Armenian Gusan" choir, having with him Armenag Shahmouradian,[78] who was in Constantinople at the time. Of course Komitas had great hopes for help from the embassy's intervention through Schmavonian. He expected this intervention to save him.[79]

It is doubtful that all the written cards arrived at their destinations.

Of course many were held back at the jail office, where they were subjected to careful scrutiny and censorship.

Komitas' hopes were very high all day and around evening time, with the sudden luck that was bestowed on Dr. Bazil Khan, Komitas' hopes were raised even more, and with him that of many others, who for similar purposes had addressed cards to influential people.

Chapter 4

The Broken Mirror and the Broken Leg

Dr. Bazil Khan was the physician of the Persian Embassy of Constantinople. He was a professor of medicine. By origin he was from Nor-Djugha and for a long time he lived in Calcutta. He was an educated, well-spoken, good-natured man. Once in a while he was published in Armenian periodicals. He wrote for *Azadamard*,[80] where he published a long-winded article on Persian-Indian Armenian communities. Most probably this article was the reason for his arrest. Usually he was not involved in politics. He also published in the conservative paper *Piuzantion*.[81] In any case, he was brought to the attention of Turkish police by Armenian secret agents.[82] Such agents were quite ignorant, estranged from the Armenian community, and compiled the majority of names from Armenian periodicals of the time. The police, as we saw earlier, did not distinguish between revolutionaries and conservatives. They arrested the whole staff of *Azadamard* – editors, administrators, even type-setters – along with Piuzant Kechian, the owner and publisher of *Piuzantion*. I have known Bazil Khan since 1908. I met him at the election of Izmirlian Catholicos in Echmiadzin. He was the delegate for Armenian communities of India and Persia.

The same morning, after roll call had finished, Kechian approached me, took out a small comb from his pocket, and handed it to me.

"Comb your hair, those bastards will see your disordered hair and think that you are scared."

Rightfully, I had not washed, and I did not have a comb, and of course my rebellious hair must have bushed up at the top of my head, which had not escaped his attention.

But of course, I was also observing his hair. It did not require special sharpness of sight to see that his hair, as well as his beard and eyebrows, which were artificially and somewhat exaggeratedly shiny black, were all white. It was obvious that in the morning, during his grooming, he lacked the little bottle which gave the thick blackness to his hair.

"In my case it is questionable, but if they observed you well last night, surely they would think that you were scared," I replied smilingly.

"Me, scared?" he objected

"Look, Doctor, you are so scared that in one night your hair turned white."

He did not even glance at the mirror and replied that even before I had said anything he knew that I would comment on his hair, and laughed.

We started to gathered around no other than our respected Dr. Torkomian and joke about the day's events, especially about the

Dr. Vahram Torkomian

growing number of those who were fearful, pessimistic, and backstabbing.

During our conversation, my fingers were fiddling with a mirror. I was trying to catch a ray of sun and shine it on someone standing close by.

Dr. Bazil, who was following my game, extended his hands to me.

"Is it broken," he observed, pointing to the mirror.

Truly the mirror was cracked.

The doctor took the mirror from my hands and for a long while his gaze was fixed on it. Later he returned it to me and said that there is a legend among Armenians of India, according to which, it is good luck to see one's face accidentally in a mirror cracked by someone else.

"And if someone gazed at a mirror that they themself broke?" I asked.

"They say it is very bad. But the fact is that I glanced at a mirror broken by someone else…Tomorrow I will get good news."

The matter did not even wait until next day. That same night the Persian Embassy succeeded in snatching Dr. Bazil Khan from jail and save him. They called him in such a hurry that he did not even have a chance to say a word to any one of us.

The news traveled from group to group, like a burning meteorite, and created lots of excitement. The story of my cracked mirror, which

I had told a few close friends, was repeated from mouth to mouth. Many wanted to look at it, yet others would fix their gaze on it hoping that the luck that befell on Bazil Khan would also befall on them. A young business man, a citizen of Persia, Theodor Mendzigian,[83] whose friends were pushing him to look at the mirror, refused, stating that the Persian Ambassador, with whom he had a close relationship before he was arrested, would not forget him. Considering that he remembered Dr. Bazil Khan, he thought that he would probably be the third person to be released.

After a while, while I was in hospital in Angora (Ankara), where they were deliberately not treating my broken leg, I heard with sorrow that Mendzigian was also not very far from the city, in the bloody valley of Mount Elma, one of the—without any exaggeration—half-alive, half-dead buried martyrs. Despite the fact that I was very reluctant to believe in such superstitions, my mind unconsciously wondered toward that cracked mirror and I thought, could it be that his unwillingness of that day played a role in what subsequently happened to him? Today I can smile at the thought, but it was something else during those days, *those black days...*

Perhaps the Persian Ambassador did not fail to intervene on his behalf but those hyenas did not let go of their prey that easily. After Mendzigian's murder, the Persian Embassy could also not prevent the temptation of the government to loot his rich department store. They most probably exiled and killed him in order to accomplish the looting.

Concerning the mirror, as I said, many who heard about what had happened now insisted on looking at their face in the mirror. For a while there were so many of them that I got annoyed, left the mirror with them, and walked away. I do not know who finally kept it.

After the departure of Bazil Khan even the most pessimistic among us started to breathe sighs of relief. Maybe there was a possibility of coming out of imprisonment. Obviously the most hopeful were foreign citizens, especially the citizens of Persia, who were many among us.

Mihrtad Haygazn, who was not very affected by his arrest nor disturbed by the possibility of exile, was yelling this way and that in his rough and deafening voice, "Let the foreign nationals prepare their bags... and wish us the same."

Ayingadji Yerevoum yelled out to one of the jail guards who was collecting the tea cups, "*Arkadash* [friend], if foreign nationals are released, don't forget us... *Biz de Hayasdanli yis* [and we are from Armenia]."

Mihrtad Haygazn

The guard, who did not understand the word "*Hayasdanli* [from Armenia]," walked away without responding to the remark. But Yerevoum's words did not leave a good impression on our friends, and many did not hide their annoyance, although internally they were thankful that he did not use the Turkish word "*Ermanisdanli*" instead of "*Hayasdanli*," as the former term would not have been missed by the guard.

"There is no need to play with fire" reprimands poured from here and there.

Yerevoum, who spent his life playing with fire, continued with notable contempt. "What can we do, my agha?" he said to someone standing closest to him in mixed Armenian-Turkish. "We are *fukhara* [poor] people, we don't have *bashkha eylendje* [other entertainment]."

Causing a disturbance, he left to join his friends, who were sitting cross-legged in a round circle in the middle of the square, about to play *barbut*.

As soon as Yerevoum disappeared, one of us, who is no longer with us, and whose name I do not wish to give, lamented, "The thing that disturbs me is not the possibility of a tragic end, but the fact that history is going to record that we were martyred with '*tulumbadjis*.'"

But those "*tulumbadjis*," whom Mikayel Shamdandjian[84] had christened with that "muscular" nickname – the word was stuck with us – on one special occasion gave an even bigger lesson to those people who had ignored them.

Later, when we were in Chankiri, the Patriarchate sent an initial sum of 140 gold liras to help the needy amongst the exiled. The arrival of that sum caused a real scandal and ugly arguments. People, who had the means and possibility to bring as much money as they wanted from Constantinople – no restrictions or limitations were imposed on this – asked for a share of the sum, which remained untouched for the whole week. Finally, a group was formed consisting of Yervant Chavoushian (Hunchagian), Taniel Varoujan (Tashnagtsagan), Stephan Tanielian (Hunchagian), and me as the representative of non-political exiles. We were entrusted with the duty of carefully examining the needs of each exiled person and to make a fair distribution. When we went to the so called *tulumbadjis*, they categorically refused to accept any aid. They even made us feel that we had hurt their pride and excused themselves.

"It will be shameful to touch the nation's money... God forbid we should need that money."

Only one among them, the one who was brought from Kadikeoy, the famous "*deveji*", whose real name I have forgotten, who was an absolutely dislikable fellow, unbeknown to others, applied and was allocated a sum. But when the others found out, they threw him out of their circle and stopped their friendship with him.

That day, when we were about to leave, Yerevoum called me, pointed to the mountains that surrounded Chankiri, and said, "Little brother, do you see these mountains... there is not a mouse hole that we don't know in them... we can run away any time we want, but we will not do it, because if we run away, they will give you a hard time... tell this to your big aghas..."

This one comment was enough for Varoujan to fall in love with Yerevoum. Next day, at his request, we went to see Yerevoum. We brought him to the coffee shop near the brook, where a few friends joined us, and Varoujan asked him to tell us in great detail a few adventures of his *ayingadji* life. Those were not small stories, but he told them with clarity, without bravado, without boasting, especially without minimizing the manliness of their natural enemy, the guards of the Tobacco Regié.

Varoujan, who was the only one among us who continued to work – *he had already written six note-books of poetry* – wanted to make Yerevoum a hero in a poem, which he really deserved. One of the stories about Ergan Mirijdan, one of his very brave friends, simply left us with the impression of an epic story. After the fall of Miridjan, the guards of the Regié not only put their guns down, but also befriended the smugglers. They performed the burial together, and to make up for the death of their brave enemy with their own bullet, they allowed the smugglers to walk away freely with the smuggled tobacco, with a sworn promise that Miridjan's portion of the profit will go to his family.

I do not know if Varoujan had time to write that verse. What was the point of writing it anyway? On the day of his martyrdom they probably opened the tiny packages of Varoujan and the meagerly belongings of the four others who accompanied him. I do not think any of them, like many of us, owned more than a shirt, a few collars, a pair of socks, and two or three handkerchiefs. They were robbed in front of Tuney Khan, where they were killed. Most probably, the real treasure in Varoujan's package, the six notebooks of poetry, which he wrote in Chankiri, were scattered to the wind. It is not known what fate befell them. But it can be assumed that the grocery store owner of the khan, Dishleg Hussein Agha, who was one of the witnesses of the crime, removed them with care, took them to the store, tore the pages, lined them up, passed a string through them, and hanged them on the wall... to wrap olives and cheese for his customers.

Immediately after the release of Dr. Bazil Khan, a new and even more resounding incident strengthened our hopes. Clerks from the jail office called Marzbed and took him away in a hurry. The general impression was that he also was released and this created even more enthusiasm than the release of Bazil Khan. After all, the doctor was a harmless man, though Marzbed was an active member of the Tashnagtsoutiun and had caused lots of grief to the government. The revolutionary was being released, while the rest were being held, even though they had no connection with the revolutionaries whatsoever. And the latter were the majority among us. There were a few of us who waited for one or two hours but he still did not return. Almost every one thought that he was also released.

But Marzbed was not freed. While we were joking around, having fun and laughing, we were not aware that in the office of the political director Reshad Bey, the chief of police Bedri Bey, the director of the central jail Ibrahim Effendi, and other police officers were busy deciding who among us was going to which destination of exile, Chankiri or Ayash. Both of these places were unfamiliar to us, and each one of us was already assigned to one. They had called Marzbed in for interrogation and they had held him down while setting us on our journey. Only on the night of Monday May 3rd, 1915, after our departure, the 28 newly arrested men were sent to Angora, where they were all jailed. While our large group was transported courtesy of the government, they had charged the 28 men in the central jail 192 ghurush and 10 para for their transport expenses.

On Friday May 7th, 16 out of the 28 jailed, one of whom was Roupen Sevag, were put on the road to Chankiri where they joined us. That same day they took out the remaining 12 men, boarded three carts during heavy rain, and transported them to Ayash. Among this latest group was also Marzbed. The fact that he was not released was unknown to us as I mentioned, and his circumstances as we imagined them were very encouraging to us. Those who had put their hope on outside intervention were able to shake away their fears. Dr. Torkomian, the most hopeless among us, was simply transformed. He was the personal physician of Prince Medjid and hoped to be saved by him. At one point this hope was so pronounced in him that he did not hide his intention to intervene on behalf of Komitas in front of Prince Medjid.

"What the Vartabed [Komitas] did for me last night by staying up is not something that one forgets. He was like a guardian angel who gave me support and dispersed my anguish which could have led me to despair... without him I could not stand up on my feet today."

As it is known, Prince Medjid was the last Caliph of the Muslim world but he was without a throne. The sultanate had already been abolished. Later, by the order of Mustapha Kemal,[85] the prince was exiled to Nice where he lived and eventually died. He was very fond of arts and if I am not mistaken he painted and highly appreciated Komitas. Once he attended a concert given by Komitas. He admired and honored him by inviting him to his palace. Komitas sang and played for him in the palace. The prince gave him his autographed photo, which is presently kept at the Nubarian Library [in Paris].

In the evening the echo of the intense shelling at the Straits inspired us with hope and we could not remain indifferent to events. The most wonderful liberty could have resulted from that shelling. Some among us thought that the government on the day of its escape would take us along to Konya or somewhere else. We could also hope that the Turks, after the fall of the capital, would stop the war and we would all be freed with them.

Komitas, who loved to create words, threw the word *"rmperk"* [song of bombs] in the air, which soon became very popular. Others attached the "tri-voice" adjective to it, alluding to the three allied forces: Russian, British and French. For a long while nobody spoke of anything else but the "three part rmperk," which was getting louder as time passed. The guards were disturbed as much as we were, or even more. All of them were out of their dens, visibly upset, gathered together in a corner. They were listening to the shelling carefully, without uttering a word. How

Dr. Roupen Sevag

different were our thoughts from theirs at that moment which did not last very long.

The thunder of the shelling was not over when a few of the guards started to loudly call the names of all who had received packages from outside.

Piuzant Kechian, Dr. Torkomian, Jacques Sayabalian and many others whom I do not remember, surely the ones who sent telegrams, disappeared for a while with the policemen and then returned one by one. First came Kechian, who was carrying a huge mattress. He went directly to Subyan Mektebi to settle for the night. He took that bed with him all the way to Chankiri. Following him was Dr. Torkomian. Not able to carry the bed that they had sent him from his house, a young man who was not familiar to us was carrying it for him. They also went toward the Subyan Mektebi.

Then Jacques Sayabalian appeared holding a tray covered with a white towel. His wife had brought him food. One of the most pessimistic among us, the poor man looked so oppressed, as if he lacked the energy to carry that light but appetizing burden from the police station. I, Krikor Yesayan[86] and Gigo, who were beside me, hurried to see him. No sooner than he saw us, Sayabalian extended the tray to

Gigo and said, "Take this, I am so emotional that I will not be able to eat anything…"

We tried to encourage him but it was impossible to change anything in his dark thoughts. Perhaps he felt condemned to death. Despite the effort to disperse those thoughts out of his head, he left the tray in Gigo's hand and hurriedly walked away.

"What are we to do?" said Gigo, "I took the tray from his hands. I was concerned that he would drop it."

"Let us keep it," interjected Krikor Yesayan. "He might calm down and change his mind in a while."

But Sayabalian refused to eat anything later as well. The tray that was brought in by Mrs. Sayabalian was left for the three of us. Appetite was not something we lacked. The only thing we did not touch were two huge oranges. One of those we peeled and fed Sayabalian almost by force. The other one he left for us.

Chapter 5

Sunday in Jail

Many of us began to think that we might be held in the central jail for a long time. Whoever thought about it assumed that each of us would have a mandatory court hearing. Even if the result was exile, only those who could possibly be accused of anything would be exiled. The fact that among us were many completely innocent people who had kept distant from any national activities led to our mistaken assumptions.

It was true that for a few hours no new prisoners were brought in, and there were a few missing people whose absence was completely puzzling.

For example, [Yervant] Odian, Hagop Der Hagopian, Sirouni, Chifte-Saraf, Alexander Panosian, and many others whose names were called during the readings of the lists were absent. There were also many other community activists from different areas, such as Ghazaros Haladjian and Nerses Ohanian, who belonged within our ranks more than outside. But we thought that they were able to hide or were waiting in police stations to be escorted to jail.

In any case, no one thought that even if we were going to be exiled as a group, that the exile would take place that same night. The reason for this was that only a few hours earlier we were permitted to write letters to our homes and ask for the delivery of necessities. These letters, considering the Ottoman post's reputation as a turtle nest in terms of speed, would reach their destinations, at the earliest, by the following Monday evening.

Considering our safety, before the fall of dark, we took advantage of the freedom that we enjoyed around the jail and started to make arrangements among ourselves for the choice of cells. We were trying to prevent arguments breaking out because they would be followed by new opportunities for the intervention of the guards.

The latter were not interested in our business. All of them were busy making money – renting beds and pillows, even for less than the night before. The beds that were rented earlier for five ghurush were now three ghurush, and it was possible to have clean pillows, only used by three or at the most four customers, plus a pillow-cover that could still pass for white, for two ghurush. The pillows in general were very big and could serve in case of need as beds.

Many benefited from this drop in price. The guards collected the money and marked down the names of people on a piece of paper, with a promise to deliver the beds after supper. They were simply laughing at us. They knew while making these offers that during the night, immediately after supper, they would take us on the road. They were trying to swindle us as much as they could. But we, as I said earlier, did not doubt their words and were trying to continue to work on the arrangement of cells as expediently as possible.

Hagop Djololian (Sirouni)

The official room of the jail, which was disposed to a few of us the night before, was left for our use. With the departure of Dr. Bazil Khan there was now room available for one person. Upon Kelegian's suggestion, that place was allocated to Komitas Vartabed, who had been obliged to spend the whole previous night with Dr. Torkomian. Komitas not only had hardly slept but had also been very disturbed by the cigarette smoke of others who had also remained awake. If he spent most of the day in the courtyard of the jail leaning his back to this or that tree, it was to stay as far away as possible from the smoke of the cigarettes.

Kelegian proposed to rent a pillow and a first class bed for the vartabed, because the beds were also divided into "A" and "B" classes. I saw this in a number of other jails as well. The jail guards gave the name "*Insiz yatagh*" (uninhabited bed) to the A-class beds, which simply meant there were no bedbugs in them, and of course those were rented for double the price. But Komitas, as it is known, did not care to sleep on a soft surface. He declined the bed but did not refuse the pillow.

Two more places remained available in the same room because Dr. Miskdjian and his pharmacist brother preferred to transfer to Subyan Mektebi.

"Over-there," the doctor said, alluding to his tall stature, "at least I can extend my feet as I like, without putting them in one or another person's mouth, as it happened here."

Although he did not say, we already knew that he had put one of his toes in Dr. Dikran Allahverdi's mouth, and because of that, an incident had taken place. Dr. Allahverdi, an active Ittihadist, could not accept the blow from the party which he served, and it hurt his pride. He had now become an unpleasant person.

Yervant Odian

"Man, they play this *oyin* [game] on me," he said, "but I will be released, you will see… I sent a direct telegram to Talaat… *Merkezi Umumi* [the general headquarters] as well… I will not stay long…"

He was right. He was going to be freed, but a little later, not until after his exile to Ayash.

One of the vacant spaces created by Miskdjian's departure was occupied by Balakian Vartabed and the other was allocated to Father Housig Kachouni from Arapkir. Incarceration and exile were not new experiences for this white-haired old man. He had a taste of jail during the Hamidian regime.

The arrangements for the other cells did not pass as smoothly and gave rise to a few small disagreements but fortunately they were soon resolved. People who were close to each other or did not want to separate from each other desired to stay as a group in one or the other jail. This task encountered some difficulties because many insisted on not moving from the jail or corner where they had lounged the night before. People simply did not want to leave their "warm corner," as they said, to others.

To solve these arguments Mihrtad Haygazn played a providential role. Starting in the morning, partly due to his deep appreciation of life in jail, and even more because of his deafeningly loud voice, Haygaz asserted authority even in the eyes of jail guards. Wherever there were disagreements or arguments, he would squeeze his huge belly in between the people arguing and destroy, or better to say, quash them. He would sometimes do this with sweet words, but more often with loud obscenities – to which he possessed the art to giving a tender tone – and thus succeed in convincing one or the other party to restore the peace.

Our people from Pera, who had been brought in late the night before and had felt very uncomfortable in this or that corner of the *govoush* (prison wing), rushed to conquer a corner in Subyan Mektebi early on, exactly under the lamp post of the entrance which at the same time illuminated part of the main hall. There was a place saved for me near them. They occupied this corner, taking advantage of the absence of the people who had occupied the space the night before. To prevent the latter from reoccupying the same place, they alternatively left two men to guard the spot. The others went and complained to the jail guards, but the guards, knowing that we were going to be exiled that same night, did not want to get involved and told them they should not have abandoned their place. The people had despaired and had returned with the intention of using crude force but they were out of luck because the turn to guard the spot had passed on to Gigo and Krikor Yesayan. Gigo was a weak man and if you blew on him, he would fall over. But Krikor Yesayan was a sturdy, broad shouldered young man, with short arms, and a real boar. He alone was able to confront the attackers, a few of whom were quite messed up when we hurried towards them with Mihrtad Haygazn.

The latter was a friend of the people from Pera, and he soon found a way to bring out the injured parties and to lead them gently to the govoush.

Chapter 6

The Wolves and the Coachman

This incident was an opportunity for me to enter the Subyan Mektebi for the first time and to glance around the general scene after the resolution of the conflict. The building was made of wood and consisted of a small entrance hall into a larger hall, which was the main school, with a few rows of desks still standing at the end. In ordinary times, that room did not serve as sleeping-quarters for the adolescent inmates. Their dormitory was in the nearby two-level stone building, and only their bathrooms were open for our use. All the windows were securely fortified with iron trellises.

Our people from Pera had occupied the passage-way on the left and right corners between the two halls, attracted by the light from the lamps hanging just in the middle. Beside the ones on the left corner, the length of the wall were lined by familiar faces, Yervant Chavoushian, Mikayel Shamdandjian, Abraham Hayrigian, Shavarsh Krisian, composer Miridjan Artinian,[87] the armsdealer Mgrdich Barsamian. There were also from the Hunchagians Sako, Bedros Kalfayan, Ardzrouni and Stepan Tanielian. There were empty spots, whose occupants, of course, were outside. Two of these, having heard the news of the discord, suddenly appeared to make sure their spots were not occupied by others. One of them was Kris Fenerdjian, who was a main culprit in the [1904] Yildiz bomb incident and was known more familiarly by the pseudonym of Silvio Ricci. The other was the famous *Cholakh* Artin from Rodosto, the tenant of Pangalti Cemetery's Armenian coffeehouse, which, for us, and of course for the many liberal minded youth from Pera, and no doubt for a bunch of Armenian secret agents, was the common gathering place before our arrests.

Just facing them, on the right side of the small hall, Dr. Torkomian and Piuzant Kechian had laid down their beds side by side. The latter had spread his bed at its width, because he was going to lay in it with his brother-in-law, Dr. Misak Djevahirian who, like him, was a big bellied man. A few pharmacists were also settled down on that side,

Avedis Zarifian, Hagop Nargiledjian, Asadour Arsenian, Hagop Terzian, as well as architect Simon Melkonian, engineer-agronomist Nshan Kalfayan and others, of whom I remember only two merchants, Teodor Mendzigian and Noyig Der Stepanian. Almost all of them had rented beds from the jail guards the night before.

The main hall was half empty at that moment because many were in the jail's square. But at the top end of the hall, the senior leaders of the Tashnag party had taken their places, Agnouni, Karekin Khajag, Haroutiun, Roupen Zartarian, Siamanto, Sarkis Minasian, Hayg Tiryakian, Dr. Garabed Pashayan, Haroutiun Kalfayan and perhaps others I do not remember.

They were separated from the remaining inmates of the hall because of the few desks which were not removed. The seats and bookstands of these desks were being used as beds for a few people, most probably for junior members

Haroutiun Shahrigian (Adom)

of the Tashnag party, because two members, Artin Misirlian and Armenag Arakelian, who I think were workers at *Azadamard* newspaper, were watching over them as guards.

Komitas, Dr. Torkomian, and a close relation of the latter, Yetvart Boyazian, who was one of the pillars of the working home of the Tashnag party, had spent the night between two desks.

The abovementioned senior group of Tashnag party members, apart from roll call and the time allocated to write letters, isolated themselves in that corner and remained generally sad and taciturn. Only Khajag and Sarkis Minasian left their circle to make a tour amongst others to gather rumors.

Khajag was personally pessimistic of the final outcome of events, but he kept his cool and we never saw him yielding. In general he smiled and uttered sweet words, and it was a pleasure to listen to him. He had a well developed gift of the gab. Like all demagogues, he was inspired by the masses, as the masses were inspired by him. I do not forget the big commotion created by his words at Zavarian's funeral, at Sourp Yerortoutiun (Holy Trinity) Church in Pera, where the huge courtyard was filled with a massive crowd, entirely consisting of the cream of Constantinople's Armenian youth.

Khajag described the cruel life that was the lot of each one of them, often spent in jails and exile, persecuted and driven away, always obliged to be wary of one's own shadow. Suddenly he addressed his words to the youth who were listening to him attentively and in a respectful silence, and he said, or more correctly, he whispered, almost as a murmur with a helpless voice, "Live, young men... but do not live like us."

The place, the occasion, the circumstances, the stress of the voice, gave such power to these simple words that everybody was shaken and, for a while, a spontaneous rustling noise arose

Khajag (Karekin Chakalian)

from everywhere, like the dying echo of thunder. All eyes were fixed on him, and all of them were overflowing with tears. Some were sobbing.

In jail, of course, we sometimes saw him with a morose face, almost in a dreamlike state. Most probably, at those moments, he was thinking of his young ones, as he liked to call his two beautiful and especially lovely daughters, Nvart and Araxi, better known to those close to him as Nunus and Alos.

These emotionally charged moments were very rare and in general he remained calm and undisturbed, without disguising his pessimism, but thinking with courage about what happened and what was going to happen. He would say that we would fall, but that we were not the important ones, because the cause for which we were going to fall was going to be victorious.

He had a story about a Russian official and during that single day he repeated that story perhaps ten times to different people. A few times he repeated it to us, without recalling that he had already told us the story. That official, while traveling on a sledge, was followed by a hungry pack of wolves. As the wolves came closer, he yelled to the coachman about the danger, that the wolves were close, that they would hash him. The coachman turned his head, looked at the wolves which were really close, and said, "It's nothing." He shrugged his shoulders and continued to whip the horses. The wolves came even closer and a few of them jumped onto the sleigh. The official once more yelled at the coachman, who again turned his head, looked at the wolves, and said again, "It's nothing," shaking his shoulders and continuing to crack his whip on the back of the horses. The wolves finally succeed in pulling down the servant of the official who was sitting beside the coachman. This time, before the official had time to scream, the coachman turned around and yelled with the full force of his lungs, "This is nothing either." As the wolves started to hash the poor man, he let the coach loose, waved his whip in the air as a sign of victory, and arrived at the village where they were going to spend the night.

After relating this story, Khajag invariably repeated that our cause would also achieve its victory, in a more assured way, even if a few people became food to the wolves of that day.

Sarkis Minasian was undisturbed and did not think much about the events of the day. Of course, he did not have confidence in the Ittihad party and the government it formed, but he was very far from imagining that they could commit criminal acts.

"The problem is, where are they going to isolate us," he said with the conviction that the government's wish was to keep the leading elements of the Armenian nation under close control, to make them absolutely dysfunctional for a while, probably until the end of the war.

We learned from him that Agnouni always believed that Talaat would intervene, insisting that their arrest was a result of a simple misunderstanding and that sooner or later they would be freed.

He harbored such beliefs and maintained a very benevolent, even very respectful and affectionate relationships with well-known members of the Ittihad party – who were actually going to prove to be the most bloodthirsty in organizing the annihilation of Turkey's Armenian nation. Agnouni probably did not forget that some time before his arrest, when he was sick at home, Talaat had paid him a personal visit to offer his good wishes. During usual discussions,

Agnouni liked to refer to "Our Talaat" every time he had an opportunity to do so.

For many years our Russian-Armenian brothers, who played with the fate of Turkey's Armenians, did not comprehend Turkish ways, even though such understanding was the foremost requirement before embarking on their dangerous game. The Turks took advantage of their lack of knowledge on every occasion, always with a smile on their faces, courteous and friendly in their relations, glazing honey on their words. These were of course civilized persons' characteristics, but if they knew Turkish ways, they would have known instantly that there was a difference between civilized men and these civilized Turks.

Krikor Zohrab

Agnouni kept his conviction about Talaat unchanged until Ayash concentration camp. He even made an attempt for the release of the whole group with a telegram appealing to Talaat's kindness. The latter did not answer. More correctly, his answer was the conviction of Agnouni, Khajag, Roupen Zartarian, Dr. Daghavarian, Sarkis Minasian and Haroutiun Djangulian by the Diyarbekir Military Tribunal which amounted to a death sentence.

Diyarbekir's famous Military Tribunal was active at a time when the whole country was subject to a siege mentality, and the job of justice was naturally entrusted to military tribunals. But I do not know who Diyarbekir Military Tribunal convicted, and who was put on their way there to be convicted. Zohrab[88] and Vartkes were going to be convicted in Diyarbekir, Carmen as well, and of course many others. But none of them reached Diyarbekir, as in the case of Agnouni and his five friends, who were murdered in Karajurun.

Only on the day when Agnouni left Ayash did he understand, finally, his mistake, and he made a heartbreaking call, by stating that he did not care about being murdered, because as a man he was destined to die anyway. "But" he added "it hurts me that we were tricked by those rascals."

Amongst others we learned from Sarkis Minasian of Siamanto and Roupen Zartarian's blackest despair. Minasian revealed that Shahrigian was the most taciturn and kept replying to even direct questions with an unchanging answer, "He gave his opinion earlier." According to Minasian, Shahrigian was amongst the despaired with Dr. Garabed Pashayan who, although had a Persian passport, did not believe that the people at the head of government who freed Dr. Bazil Khan would make a new concession for the Persian consul. The only hopeful one in the group was Haroutiun Kalfayan,[89] owing to his close links to Turkish circles.

Vartkes
(Hovhannes Serengulian)

Roupen Zartarian was in a truly troublesome state the previous night. He had come to jail sick with a heavy case of dysentery and was left sleepless until morning, obliged to go out many times. The school had no toilets and for that reason he had to go to the adjoining stone building's basement. That was some task. Each time he had to explain himself to the jail guards, who did not like to be disturbed too much. The guards were obliged to accompany him back and forth.

Melkon Gurdjian was in the same corner with this group, but he spent the entire day outside with us. He had many acquaintances and liked to chat. Jail and exile were not a novelty in his life. We always saw him in a happy mood. He joked with this or that person and even sang love songs in Armenian or Turkish from his native Palu folk songs.

Chapter 7

Midnight! Lanterns Lit the Court-Yard

Before the fall of darkness a new bread distribution took place. By and large the jail cells were abandoned and the crowd was again dispersed in the square. Only a few were to have an illusion of supper – those who during the day had the foresight to buy food from the jail grocer and to save it for later. The majority were obliged to be satisfied with bread only. The grocer had closed his store, announcing that he had nothing left to sell.

A few people without paying any attention to this rumor, insisted on going to the grocer, but all of them returned empty handed. The last group that returned brought worrisome news. The grocer was obviously disturbed by the repeated inquiries and questions and felt obliged to give an answer. To put an end to the harassment once and for all he had told them that he would not receive any new supplies before the morning, and that he was doubtful that the morning supplies would be of any use to us. It had not been possible to get more clarification from him. Mihrtad Haygazn, who was with the last group, concluded that we were simply going to be taken away that same night.

"These things always start like this," he said with a definitive accent.

Soon suspicions started to spread among the other groups.

Those who had money tried to convince the guards to bring supplies from outside, of course with the promise of reward, but the guards who up to then had never missed an opportunity to make a profit refused with the excuse that it was already night-time and they could not go out either.

As credible as that argument sounded, nobody was convinced, and suspicions remained amongst a few prisoners. The latter went around murmuring, "Something is going on." At the time, these people were not that many, but soon, when more than a dozen jail guards came out of the basement of the govoush, each holding a burning lantern and starting to hang them from the trees, others also became suspicious that "certainly something was going on." Indeed was there a need to illuminate the square if, after a short while, everyone was going to their cells to spend the night behind closed doors?

Even Yerevoum's group, whose members had experience in jail, started to look worried.

"I cannot comprehend the reason for this *donanma* (festive illumination)," remarked one of them.

Parsegh Shahbaz

A little further from them, two other jail specialists, Mihrtad Haygazn and Smpad Piurad were having a serious argument. This was not the first argument between them since the morning. Mihrtad insisted that they would be exiled that same night and he advised people around him not to undress and to be ready for any eventuality. But Piurad was of the opinion that we would stay in the central jail for a long time, until such time as others who were still outside had joined us. Neither one nor the other's opinion was based on convincing proof. They argued solely on assumptions, and because there was no possibility of getting information, we preferred to withdraw to our cells. The other groups, who were further away, did the same thing without an awareness of our discussions.

On our way back to Subyan Mektebi, we were joined by a group of junior Tashnag party members. Among them were Kegham Parseghian, Parsegh Shahbaz, Dikran Cheogiurian, Khachig Idaredjian and Yenovk Shahen. All of them were aware of the suspicions and they also believed that we could be exiled that same night. Noticeably the first two had a worried look about them.

Kegham Parseghian, even before his arrest, saw everything in black. He had known that lists were being prepared in different districts of Constantinople and addresses were being verified at city offices. He had the enduring premonition that not only would he be arrested but also that he would have a tragic faith. During the day among his friends he was the most despaired and was almost completely silent.

Shahbaz was as pessimistic but showed lots of courage in comparison. Like many others, he also had the conviction that finally, in Constantinople or somewhere else, each one of us would be interrogated. Some expected their release after such a trial. Shahbaz, to the contrary, was afraid.

"I do not think that they arrested me for just being a party member," he said. "If all party members were to be arrested, there would not be any space to drop a pin in this huge jail."

He believed that all of us were arrested for being active in different fields. He ascribed his pessimism about his own fate to a mission he was implicated in Kharpert[90] after the re-establishment of the constitution. He had thus alienated Turkish functionaries who became his enemies.

"Only Rashid is enough," he added, alluding to the chief-of-police in Mezre; Rashid Bey from Kesreg, who was going to destroy Kharpert.[91] Poor Shahbaz was going to fall in this man's hands as well.

Hampartsoumian, an innocent young man, without much experience, who almost did not believe in any wickedness, had fewer dark thoughts. He missed his family a lot. He had just married Siamanto's sister, and his only concern was that the adventure we were embarking on would not last long.

Cheogiurian, although pessimistic, was talkative. Yenovk Shahen and Krikor Yesayan never left his side all day, and he caught the cheerfulness of one or the other, whenever there was an occasion to laugh. The occasions were plenty throughout the day.

Two truly careless people remained in this group: Khachig Idaredjian and Yenovk Shahen. The first could be counted among the people arrested by mistake. The mistake was not the policemen's doing. The police had come to take away his older brother. Khachig, thinking about the long years that his brother had spend in the jails of Abdul Hamid wanted to spare his elder brother the pain of a new imprisonment. Without saying anything to his family, he accompanied the policemen, telling them that he was the one they were looking for.

"He already paid his dues," he said alluding to his brother. "This time it must be my turn, considering we always walked the same path."

He did not think that his arrest would end in tragedy. He had no clue about his amazing self-sacrifice.

As for Yenovk Shahen, he simply saw the surprise gathering in the central jail as a pass-time and spent his day in a merry way. We kept hearing his giggles from this or that corner of the square.

Sunday April 25th, 1915 ended in such an atmosphere, the only full day that we were to spend in the central jail of Constantinople.

When I started to write this series of articles, I had the intention to inscribe my memories related to Komitas Vartabed and immediately go on to the circumstances under which the first symptoms of his cruel illness appeared. But when the first articles were published, friends, even readers who I did not know, asked me to widen my initial project and give a comprehensive picture of the Constantinople arrests and the exile that followed – the arrogant beginning of the 1915-1918 drama. This was the reason, for my thorough and detailed description of that one day in the central jail. There we were still together in a group and under each other's

Yenovk Shahen

surveillance. That was when we formed our first impressions of each other. These impressions could not have escaped attention and in general remained unchanged during the course of future events.

Although I have provided quotations to relate my story better and to make myself better understood, conveying a better sense of the psychological state in which we found ourselves, the picture I have drawn is far from a comprehensive one. Whatever I wrote was simply a testimony of that day's life, as some of the people were close to us or were famous. It is one testimony observed from a certain angle, reflecting one man's impressions and mood. My main effort was to *record only that day's impressions* right or wrong, without redressing them or correcting them based on hindsight.

Someone else would see the same events from a different angle.

There were many among us who felt doomed to a worse fate. Others, for whom jail and exile were not novelties, looked at these developments with a lighter attitude, and even if they were pessimistic, they thought that they would find a way to slip away once more. There were people who were weak and cried in a corner; there were careless people who laughed and enjoyed themselves in another corner; and there were confused people who felt completely out of place and gathered in the company of the famous and elite of the nation. They had no way of understanding or explaining their common fate.

In general, in the mass of people numbering more than 200, even in these disturbing times, those who saw everything in black were not more than a quarter. The remaining three-quarters restrained themselves from falling into a deep state of anxiety. Of course none of them were free of anxiety, but they were able to remain brave and not give into fear. In a few cases this brave attitude was the result of strong and unbreakable character. Others got their courage from the larger group. Most probably they would have been humiliated had they been alone or shared their fate with only a few inmates.

This scenario would be more understandable if I add that throughout the day, as much as we were in custody, nobody made us feel that we were prisoners. We were more like hosts than guest around the jail. Poor Khajag, who had tasted the ill-famed Medekh dungeon in Russia and kept those memories with special deference, including the threat of the whip of Kazak jail guards, was dumb founded with the unbridled freedom that was given us in the central jail. He was equally surprised with the way things generally functioned here. A special grocery store, coffee maker, tea and coffee ready at any desired moment, even milk: in one word the freedom to do anything, to enjoy anything, as long as one had money to pay. For the ones who had money, there were other things available as well, and this caused many rumors to circulate. On that day, of course, our thoughts and desires were very far from those kinds of things.

I can even add, without stretching the truth, that on that day in prison, we felt ourselves freer than outside, be it in our homes, be it in places where we gathered or met each other. Outside, just before the arrests, the atmosphere was intolerable. Secret police were everywhere and people stopped talking in the middle of their sentence when they saw an unfamiliar person beside them. In jail we did not have this fear. All of us spoke freely about everything and to everyone, even in a loud voice, some even in Turkish. And our comments were far from being sweetened with honey.

As I mentioned previously, throughout the day, apart from those few mandatory moments, we did not see policemen among us. We only had the jail guards supervising us, and their role was such a passive one that Mihrtad Haygazn, with his fearsome voice, ordered the guards around, telling them the order in which they should serve coffee or tea.

"First this Effendi, then the other one, then this and that one..."

Of course he gave priority to senior Tashnag party members whom he served with absolute dedication throughout that day.

Agnouni
(Khachadour Maloumian)

The jail guards not only were not offended by his orders, but they carried them out with obedience.

In that atmosphere the reversal of roles was at times comical. Even Agnouni could not help but laugh when he was buying tea after he had left the Subyan Mektebi with friends after permission to write letters had been announced. This was the first and last time Agnouni laughed that day, when he saw Mihrtad in that commanding mode.

He laughed, of course, remembering other jails, where the situation was different.

When we were about to withdraw to our cells, many among us might have thought that jail under those conditions might get better rather than worse, because it was not as bad as one might have expected. Under the circumstances, the way the day had passed was not bad. And this was the impression of all, the pessimists, optimists, and the careless.

We did not think of only one thing; that the day was not over. We did not realize how close we were to our song of elegy...

Chapter 8

Hope Amidst Gloom and Doom

When I entered the jail with the junior Tashnagtsagans, there was almost no free space left for us to occupy. The majority of people had seized some corner that they had made their own. Fortunately, the place that I was allocated was under a column. At least I could lean some place while sleeping. Khachig Idaredjian and Yenovk Shahen left their friends and sat with us. Gigo and Krikor Yesayan were waiting for them. The latter, I do not know how, was able to smuggle in, despite many searches, a big razor and was shaving a pencil. Four of them were getting ready for a game of cards, Sixty-six, which they had not been able to play throughout the day. It was obvious that they did not have any intention to sleep early. With my back to the column, I was watching Kris, who had given himself to exercise, stretching his long legs to avoid disturbing his neighbors.

The most interesting scene was on the right side of the hall. Dr. Torkomian, already in bed, was arranging his coat over his blanket, to stay warm during the night. Beside him Piuzant Kechian had taken off his pants and was about to fold and use them under his head as a pillow.

The guys beside me had stopped their game to watch this scene. They had started to deal a hand but seemed as if they were not destined to play their beloved game. Elsewhere, Kechian was finally in bed and Dr. Djevahirian was about to take off his coat when Nshan Kalfayan, who was still outside, ran in yelling, "Get up, they want us."

He could not say much more. Two jail guards who accompanied him, one holding a burning lantern, also came in at the same time and invited us to gather in the square outside the main office of the jail, without wasting time by taking our belongings with us.

The guards were showered with questions from everywhere, but they gave no answers and insisted we hurry. Uproar and confusion could be heard from the square where the inmates from the govoush had hurled themselves. We were able to leave first as we were still dressed and had nothing to carry. Kris, who was with us, for the first time mentioned the word "exile" with apparent indifference.

Others were calling each other joyfully, emphasizing that we would be released.

But the sceptics outnumbered them and ominous words could be heard.

"We will be deported."

As the crowd got bigger, we were surrounded by more uproar and confusion. There were questions raised by everyone. There were also various interpretations, often unrealistic, funny and contradictory. There was a particular moment when Mihrtad Haygazn's thunderous voice rained over all. He was caught in an argument with someone, probably Smpad Piurad.

Many who formed groups and spent the day together had gathered under this or that lantern hanging from the trees. They were waiting for their friends to go to the square outside the office. We did the same, trying to keep together all who were from Pera. Many of us had dispersed to gather information about the very disturbing invitation for a meeting, the outcome of which was not a matter of doubt anymore. We were deeply convinced that what would follow was exile. It's true, there were some among us who still believed that the reason we were called was to release us, but if such a decision was taken, the jail guards would have known about it and they would not have hesitated to express their congratulations when inviting us outside, sure in the expectation that heralding such news would earn them a generous reward.

When finally we approached the entrance to the jail office, a large crowd had already gathered in front of it. There were no lights, none whatsoever. There were many lanterns burning uselessly in the square, but nobody thought of hanging some near the door. A few specs of light were coming from the edges of the carefully drawn light-screen curtains of an office window. We could only make out the identity of a few people who shared our destiny standing close to the window. The long corridor, where the door of the jail office opened, was dark. We were obliged to pass that corridor to reach the big courtyard where we would probably be told what was going to take place next.

At a distance from the door, we desperately gazed through the darkness of that corridor with the hope of seeing something. We tired our eyes for nothing. We were quiet. There was some talking among the people in the back, and we could clearly hear Mihrtad Haygazn and Smpad Piurad whose argument was continuing.

"If they called at such an unusual time, it is to set us free," Piurad argued stubbornly.

Haygaz, who had run out of arguments and negations, was simply responding with curses.

For a moment, as Khajag passed by, he recognized me and asked if I had seen Agnouni. Upon my negative reply, he tried to break through the crowd and pass forward, of course with great difficulty. It was some task to pass in that darkness and through all the huddled people. Who knows where he was pushed in that crowd which tried to go forward regardless of the obstacles.

Roupen Zartarian

Many of us left in groups but before reaching the office door, the breathless pushing and shoving of those who followed us broke up our groups. Khajag, Agnouni and their friends who had left together, of course, were all separated from each other.

Not long after Khajag had disappeared looking for Agnouni, I noticed Roupen Zartarian beside me. Was he walking or was he being driven by the crowd? As usual he had a very discouraged look and it was obvious that he was still ill. We had no chance even to exchange a word. The crowd pushed him forward, though I was trying to resist the jostling as much as possible.

Finally we were obliged to stop. Although we were at a dead end, the hustling did not stop, and we heard the voice of winemaker Onnig, one of Yerevoum's friends, "Why are you in such a hurry," he yelled. "We are not going to a wedding!"

Those who were in a hurry believed, like Smpad Piurad, that we were called to be released. Winemaker Onnig's words, which rightfully spoke of the fate that awaited us, had a chilling effect and calmed people down.

From the place where we stopped, we could see the office door and down the corridor. Both of them were in the dark for a long while, but we were finally illuminated by a few lanterns. Some sounds could be heard coming from the front, but from the place where we stood, we could not distinguish a word.

"What did they say, what did they say?" inquired everyone.

A few had kept their light heart and the jokes started.

"Would you like to go home by cart or on foot?" somebody answered, dead serious.

"I will be a *ghush* [bird], I will fly," declared an eighty year old man, standing beside me.

I saw him for the first time because at that time the moon had started to shine and the darkness that surrounded us started to disappear.

The elderly man repeated it to everyone like a slogan, because he understood the joke literally and believed that we were going to be set free.

It seemed that he had spent the day discouraged in a corner and escaped our attention. His advanced age should have drawn our attention. But more interesting was his story that we were going to learn later.

They had arrested him in Ortakiugh [Ortakeoy], mistaking him for the famous Russian-Armenian writer, Vertanes Papazian,[92] because his name was also Vertanes Papazian. He owned a humble business on one of Constantinople's famous streets where he sold manufactured goods.

The real writer Vertanes Papazian was not in Constantinople at the time of our arrest. He was in Bucharest as the principal of the local Armenian national school. He published an article in every Sunday edition of *Azadamard.* Young Armenians from Ortakiugh, who gathered in a coffee house on Sundays, where this elderly man also frequented, would joke with him after reading *Azadamard.*

"*Aferim* [bravo] Vertanes agha, you wrote very well."

The elderly man, knowing that he shared the first and last name of the correspondent of *Azadamard,* joked back and responded that the following week he would write something even better. A nested Armenian spy in the coffee-house, who had no clue about Vertanes Papazian, concluded that the correspondent to *Azadamard* "the *devlet khayini* [traitor to the state]" publicist was this old man at the verge of his death bed, and based on a report by this spy, they arrest the poor old man and put him in our caravan.

The poor man, at that age, was going to arrive with us in Chankiri. He was freed by a kind gesture on the part of Asaf Bey and returned to his family in Constantinople.

At the time I was not familiar with his story, but his old age and humiliated state caught my attention and aroused my sympathy. Otherwise, I would have uttered a sarcastic word at his naiveness about our release. He repeated his assumption with such childish joy, just as the actual situation was taking on a very grave turn.

Diran Kelegian

We could not see what was happening near the office door, but it seemed obvious that whatever it was, it was not something encouraging. Again, there was an ill-fated hiss traveling mouth to mouth from the front.

"Things are bad," they said.

Somebody just standing behind me repeated that phrase, which struck our eardrums like steel. The voice was familiar to me. I turned back and said, "To what depths have we fallen, doctor!"

It was Dr. Daghavarian, with whom I had spent a very pleasant morning the day of our arrest on April 24th.

"The important thing now is to find out our destination," he answered.

He was alluding to the location of our exile. He had spent the whole day with Diran Kelegian and did not hide the fact that in Kelegian's opinion we were going to be taken to Konya or Angora [Ankara], adding that one or the other were not the same thing for him.

"Kelegian is simply horrified at the probability of being exiled to Konya."

When I commented that the Turks of Konya had a reputation of being kind-hearted and having good relations with Armenians living with them, he added, "But the problem is that Azmi is the governor of that place." Although Kelegian's real worry was his grave personal animosity with him, in general it would also have been advantageous for all of us to stay far away from such a rascal.

Azmi Bey really possessed a very dark reputation. He was the director of Constantinople police when Kabakji Mustafa, one of the murderers of Mahmud Shevket, had succeeded escaping the gallows by hiding in the Caucasus. Kabakji Mustafa had thoughtlessly asked for asylum on a Russian steam-ship which was on its way to Europe destined to pass through Constantinople. As soon as the steam-ship had docked at Constantinople, Azmi was informed of Kabakji Mustafa's presence on board through his spies and had the steam-ship boarded by a large group of policemen. Azmi did not pay any attention to the Russian captain's protests and succeeded in capturing Kabakji Mustafa after searching everywhere. The next day, the Russian ambassador personally intervened, demanding that Kabakji be released to his custody, but he could only receive Kabakji's corpse. Azmi said Mustafa died in jail that same night as a result of heart failure. Truly they had killed him.

The Russian ambassador created a serious diplomatic incident and to satisfy him Azmi Bey was demoted and obliged to leave Turkey and go to Egypt, where he was acquainted with the famous Hunchagian party spy, Arshavir Sahagian. Through him he was informed about the party's conference and decisions taken in Keostenja [Costanza]. Taking Arshavir with him, he returned to Constantinople, and was then sent to Konya as governor.[93] It is a known fact that Arshavir's treason was the main reason for the martyrdom of 20 known Hunchagian party leaders who were hanged.

Dr. Daghavarian left me and joined Dr. Torkomian, who had spent some time getting dressed. He looked confused and spoke to this and that person for information about what was going on.

As I mentioned, the news was not good. The joke was over. Even the carefree were driven to dark thoughts. Yenovk Shahen, the day's most jovial person, came back and stood beside me. Krikor Yesayan, another carefree person, had also stepped back from the front line.

"There are rows of bayonets everywhere," they said almost in unison.

I had no time to inquire for more details. At that moment, after they got near me, that corridor where the door of the jail office opened was flooded in its entire length by light. As far as I could see from a distance, there were soldiers lined up with rifles and fixed bayonets on both sides of the corridor. We also saw a crowd of high ranking officers in the middle of the corridor. Many were unfamiliar to me, or I could not identify them with certainty from that distance. But I recognized three of them from first glance.

One of them was the director of the political branch of the police Reshad Bey, the other was the director of the central jail Ibrahim, and the third was the police chief Bedri Bey whose evil face was familiar to me from my adolescent years. Bedri Bey used to be the secretary of the famous prosecuting judge of Pera, Tateos Refke Effendi, while I was the secretary of Meriem-Kuli Haroutiun Effendi. We were in daily contact as part of our jobs. Meriem-Kuli often had dealings with Tateos Refke Effendi.

Piuzant Kechian

Standing on the tips of our toes, we were trying to understand what they were doing. We could not see anything. Suddenly, a huge mass dispersed our group like a boulder rolling down a mountain side, passing us and blocking our view completely. It was Piuzant Kechian, his bed and his blanket on his shoulder, going to the door of the jail office without paying any attention to the complaints and some curses around him. He insisted relentlessly that he would be one of the first to be called and therefore he had to move forward.

We did not even attempt to interpret his mysterious assertion. At the same time, the jail guards and policemen standing in the front of the crowd announced that whoever's name was called should come to the door of the office.

I do not know who at that moment sang the famous song of the Turkish soldiers, *"Hey gaziler, yol gerundu* [Holy Warriors, the road is open]."

But we did not take any notice.

Surely it was one of the *ayingadjis* [tobacco smugglers].

Our drama had started and we lost interest in such small matters.

Chapter 9

Head Count 197, Ayash 73, Chankiri 124

It proved to be rather difficult to gather us together. Groups of police officers and jail guards ran here and there, calling out the same instructions, so that they could be heard everywhere. Those who were in the courtyard rushed to us. There was a special presence of police officers and jail guards in front of the govoush and Subyan Mektebi. It seemed that there were still some prisoners inside. By then there was a full moon and we could see everything clearly. People were coming out of the two buildings, and as soon as they came to the courtyard on the orders of the police, they rushed toward us. A few people had small parcels, a blanket, or a change of clothes, which had been brought to them by their families after the latter had received telegrams sent to them during the day. They were holding their belongings in their hands, obviously not having had time to wrap them.

Others had wrapped the left-overs from the evening bread distribution in their parcels, having had no time to finish eating. Their cautious attitude gave rise to a wave of laughter, not knowing that later, on the train to exile, those pieces of bread were going to play a providential role.

When nobody was left in the cells and in the courtyard, the jail guards and the police officers stood side-by-side and moved forward, creating a barrier behind us. Were they worried that some of us would hide in…. the cells?

Kechian with his bedding was driven to the left and we could see in front of us clearly. Although we were still quite far from the corridor, we could observe what was going on. The ill-omened trio of Bedri Bey, Reshad Bey and Ibrahim Effendi remained in their place. They were surrounded by a few functionaries in police and military uniforms. There were also civilian-dressed officers or secret agents. Amongst the latter only one was visible with his entire body, a short stocky man, standing beside Bedri Bey, with his head hardly reaching Bedri's chest. We could not see his face, which was hidden behind two big sheets of paper that surely listed our names. That man was going to read our names with such stupefying correct diction that we all thought he had to be an Armenian. Later we understood that our assumption was correct.

It was obvious that all of them were waiting for us to be quiet. There were hisses of discontent, complaints, and sometimes even bad language rising from here and there when some people pushed to get as close as possible to the door. The most noise was coming from people surrounding Piuzant Kechian on our left.

Everybody became quiet when a voice called out the first name. It was that chubby short man.

"Kris, *naame digeri* [other name], Silvio Ricci."

"Merit of respect," called somebody from the back, alluding to Kris Fenerdjian's revolutionary past.

And here he was with his tall statue moving forward like a column from the third or fourth row and bending to pass through the office door. We had the impression that he curved his body in order to keep his head high, so that his attempt to pass through the low threshold of the door would not be mistaken as a bow. Soon he quickly passed the corridor and walked past Bedri Bey and the people surrounding him. He disappeared instantly, as if by the hand of a magician.

The senior Tashnagtsagan party members were next to be called among others. Agnouni, Khajag, Shahrigian, Roupen Zartarian, Sarkis Minasian followed suit. With them were also a few others whom I do not remember. Perhaps Rostom Rostomiants from Alexandropol? He grew up in Constantinople. He was a businessman who carried a Russian passport and did not belong to any political party. He stayed away from national affairs but was arrested by the police, mistaken for a famous Tashnag party member, the revolutionary Rostom. At the time they did not realize their mistake, neither afterwards. They were not going to undo their mistake and Rostom Rostomiants was going to be killed with a bullet in a place called Ayash Belli, an hour and a half from Ayash exile camp, on August 3rd, 1915, with 23 of his exiled friends.

Many of us thought that he was one of the Tashnagtsagan friends. Not many people knew Rostom personally. The *iants* suffix of his name smelled revolutionary, and the initial call of the pure revolutionaries' names renewed hopes among some of us that this night time action was intended to separate the revolutionaries and anti-government people from others. It is so true that one's heart does not cease to hope.

This hope, as misplaced and incredible as it was, spread with the speed of a bullet, from one person to another, specially among those who had no ties to revolutionaries and had stayed away from national affairs.

The above mentioned men disappeared with the same speed as Kris disappeared after entering the corridor. Then, when our turn came, only then we understood the reason for that mysterious disappearance. At the half-way point of the corridor, where Bedri and Reshad Beys stood surrounded by their functionaries, there were a group of policemen, and every time one of the summoned men approached them, they opened their ranks and after letting the men out to the backyard of the office, they reunited and closed their ranks. From where we stood, we could not see this operation. Even the policemen were invisible to us.

The reading of the first list, faster and faster, took more than half an hour. As the crowd of those summoned got bigger, it became easier for the remaining men to move forward. They were successively followed by famous people, writers, teachers, publicists, doctors, businessmen and others... as well as some unfamiliar people. Later came more revolutionaries, mainly Hunchag party members, junior Tashnag party members, and after them a few senior Tashnag party members. Following those immediately were printer Haroutiun Asadourian, and the other Haroutiun Asadourian, the municipal dog catcher of Constantinople who was arrested by mistake. This mistake was not corrected either, despite the fact that both names were registered side by side on the list.

The hope among those of us that the revolutionaries would be separated from our ranks was gradually fading as other types of people were being called. That false hope was completely gone when two well known anti-revolutionaries, Arisdages Kasbarian and Dr. Avedis Nakkashian, were called as well. The latter was a fascinating man who was a source of joy for people around him throughout the day.

Every time a summoned man was slow to move because he had not heard his name called out, those who were at the front row repeated the name loudly from mouth to mouth until the right man heard and moved towards the office door.

In a different mood this could have aroused many jokes. But as I said earlier, the joke was over and the drama had begun. Finally, our dealing with the wretched jail guards was over and we were facing the three functionaries of that awful regime. Although we were far, we still could see clearly. The chief of police, Bedri Bey, was examining each of the men called with a piercing, wicked look, as they passed in front of him. Given the mood we had resigned ourselves to, it was not difficult to interpret the meaning of that nasty look. And if he personally knew the people called, sarcasm and intimidation took over the satanic smile on his face.

In this first group were all those who were destined to go to the Ayash camp. There were other people other than myself counting, one-by one, those who were called. The total number did not pass 71.

In a funny coincidence, from those 71, the last two were Mihrtad Haygazn and Smpad Piurad, who did not stop arguing with each other throughout the day. The winner was Mihrtad Haygaz, who was one of the first to insist that this adventure was going to end in exile. After the incident with the grocer of the jail, he was again the first one who insisted that we would be exiled that same night. He had even warned

Dr. Avedis Nakkashian

people to be prepared for any eventuality and not to undress. Piurad, for his part, always insisted on the opposite, even when developments left no doubt about the fate that was going to fall upon us.

When the reading of the first list ended we were given a fifteen minute break. The police chief stayed where he was in an animated discussion with the chief of the central jail, Ibrahim. From the looks of things Bedri Bey was giving instructions because Ibrahim was standing in a respectful way, his two hands resting on his belly, constantly nodding his head to show that he was following the instructions. Standing beside Bedri Bey was that chubby man who had read from the list. His face remained invisible to us because he continued to cover it with that sheet of paper.

This short break gave rise to another tide of hope, that the men who were called were the ones to be exiled, and that the rest of us would remain in jail. Those few, who suddenly harbored feelings of hope, started to think that we might be set free. They did not notice that the man who read the first list was standing put, and in his hand was a second sheet of paper.

Soon it was our turn, as the man started to read our names. The first name called was Diran Kelegian, followed by the three vartabeds, Krikoris Balakian, Hovnan Garabedian and Komitas, exactly in that order. Soon came government and community functionaries, doctors, pharmacists, writers, publicists, businessmen, simple tradesmen, and with them a group of unfamiliar people, among them the *ayingadjis* in their entire group.

Kechian was one of those called early on. Finally it was my turn and I entered that narrow corridor. Passing through was not an easy matter, even without a backpack, because one had to rub shoulders with the soldier-guards who stood on both sides, making it impossible to pass without touching them. I wondered how Kechian passed through with his wide shoulders and huge bedding.

When I reached the officers' front, I tried to see the face of that chubby man who continued reading from the list, but he kept his face covered by that sheet of paper.

When I arrived at the courtyard after passing the police officers, I was told that he was Armenian. Some managed to see him when it had been impossible for me, and some knew him. They knew him as "Hidayet", by his Turkish name, and they said he had converted to Islam. I never had the opportunity to meet him before, but I remembered vaguely that before our arrest, this man was considered a well known and dangerous spy, as were Haroutiun Megerdichian, Hmayag Aramyants, and Arshavir Sahagian. Hidayet and Megerdichian played a major role in the preparation of our list of names. Aramyants did not participate in this work, mainly because he was not a police spy. He was attached to the military and mainly betrayed his friends who were party members. Sahagian, although a police spy, denounced mainly Hunchagian enemies.

Hidayet and Megerdichian caused a lot of harm to Armenians during the entire war. When Patriarch Zaven was exiled to Musul, the government attached Hidayet to the police officers watching over him. Megerdichian had a major role in the preparation of a large illustrated book, "The Ambitions and the Activities of Armenian Revolutionary Committees", in Turkish and French languages, with the help of a young Turkish journalist Asaf Bey. Both of them came to Aleppo with that special assignment. Megerdichian went on to Ourfa to include in the volume the history of the Armenian self-defense in that city, an event which he presented as an insurgency, so that the authorities could justify the massacre that had taken place there.

We remained in the courtyard of the office for a while, until all the remaining prisoners joined us. We were informed by the earlier arrivals that the group assigned to Ayash boarded special military fire trucks and left. The doors were wide open and when I arrived, one of those trucks, surely the last one, which I could clearly see, left at that moment. We could not know where they were going.

Mikayel Shamdandjian

Our group was more numerous than the first one. We had 51 more people. The calculations during the day brought our total number to 197. The courtyard of the office, as large as it was, was filled to capacity, and many climbed on the stairs leading to the first floor. Some were sitting and others were standing. Dozens of policemen, standing at different corners, were guarding us, but they were not given reason to intervene. We did not dare to ask for any information, knowing that the big beasts were inside, and no doubt the soldiers were scared of their presence and careful not to talk to us.

The last ones who joined our group were Mikayel Shamdandjian, and a young fellow from Uskudar, Haroutiun Kalfayan, who was mistaken for a Tashnag party activist, the mayor of Makri Keoy [Bakirkeoy], Haroutiun Kalfayan.

The latter had already gone with the first group to Ayash. After finding Kalfayan the Tashnag party member, nobody thought of letting this young fellow who was arrested by mistake to go free. He was a very kind character and won all of our hearts in Chankiri. No one, neither us, nor him, could ever understand why he was sent to Chankiri while the other Kalfayan was sent to Ayash. Both of them were going to be killed, the real Haroutiun Kalfayan with the last group in Ayash, and this one, arrested by mistake, with the first group that left Chankiri.

Chapter 10

The Conductors of a Requiem: Ibrahim, Reshad and Bedri

When no more people were left in the jail and all of us were in the courtyard, we were left alone for a while and this again gave rise to feelings of uncertainty. We were far away from the door and could not hear what was being said at the front. We also lost interest. Restlessness had set in us. Knowing very well that something was waiting *outside* and that *something* was the danger – unknown but nevertheless threatening – we yearned to go out without waiting any longer. We waited to be free from this uncertainty and to surrender to whatever was to be. In that waiting, we were becoming more and more irritable with the passing of each minute.

Just at that moment the policemen from the corridor descended to the courtyard. We squeezed on two sides to open a passage for them. They passed row by row, advanced to the door, and went out. They were followed by the soldiers guarding the corridor. Their bayonets were fixed to their rifles and two sub-commissioners followed them. They also went to the door and disappeared. Four police officers covered the outside view. Even those prisoners who stood in the first row said that they could not see anything. We feared falling into the same uncertainty again. However, this time we did not have to wait for long. Two new policemen came down the corridor followed by a senior police officer. Two other policemen accompanied the latter.

As soon as the latter disappeared, the policemen guarding the door invited us to come out, no doubt based on an order that they had received. We were more than 100 people, 122 to be exact. It was not an easy task coming out. Each person was trying to exit as soon as possible. Disorder reigned so badly that the policemen had to interfere without using any force. Finally we came out. The first thing that struck us was the lack of trucks or carriages. Then we had a chance to look around the wide street where we gathered in disarray. The two sides of the streets were lined by soldiers. Only some of them had come from inside. Others were already there or had come anew.

Their bayonets were fixed to their rifles. For the first time, at that moment, I observed with horror the shape of bayonets. Some of them were serrated like a saw, and a cold shiver went through my body. Later, during my unending years of exile, I saw many bayonets like that, which the Germans had introduced to the Ottoman army. Anybody wounded with that bayonet had a slim chance of surviving. The defeated Turkish soldiers in Palestine, when they retreated to Aleppo, were generally armed with those bayonets.

In the courtyard we had clearly seen two sub-commissioners watching over the soldiers, but here there were six of them, assuming we saw them all. At the far end of the streets there was a group of officers. They were quite far from us. It was possible that among them were sub-commissioners or commissioners as well. The sub-commissioners who were close to us were followed by a few soldiers like shadows. Following an order that they received, the soldiers and sub-commissioners tried to organize us in rows, which took a significant amount of time. They lined us in fours and pushed us to the front toward the officers. The sub-commissioners, all graduates of Harbiye Military College, were fervent Ittihadists and nationalists and did not have the tact of the police officers. In general, with the soldiers following them, they did not spare neither force nor curse words. In those long minutes, they used different tactics, sometimes sarcasm but more often malicious rant. Words like "*ulan,*" "*keratas,*" "*abdal*" and "*pez*" [rude street expressions] resonated many times. This lasted until they succeeded to bring our disorderly crowd, which had no clue about military discipline, into properly arranged lines. The orders issued by them were either not understood or not followed due to the unwillingness of a few of us. In those instances the sub-commissioners were forced to interfere. I do not forget how one of the soldiers had to forcefully shake me like a rag until he managed to put my feet in line. Of course I was not an exception in that regard.

After all that order, it became obvious that we were going to go some place on foot rather than on trucks. But where?

One of us noted that the direction in which we were heading was the newly built Rose-alley.

"From there, the port of Serayburnu is a few steps."

This destination uttered by the man was repeated from line to line and descended like frozen dew on our ears. Serayburnu truly enjoyed a bad reputation in the history of the Ottoman Empire. Women, who had fallen from grace in the harem of the old palace, or discredited functionaries, were tied in bags and thrown into the sea. During the Hamidian era that reputation was well alive and even sadder. Serayburnu was considered a usual slaughter place of the Turkish liberal youth. Whether true or false, the rumors maintained that such bags were filled with pieces of lead or iron when the victims were thrown in the sea. After the re-institution of the Ottoman constitution, inter-communal memorial services were held at Serayburnu in the presence of hojas and Armenian, Jewish and Greek clerics, all standing side by side.

Many of us were aware of those horrendous stories, and those who were not aware learned from others. Everybody was in distress. This was the main subject of conversation. Nobody could speak of anything else. A few who were given to despair were crying.

Soon, the soldiers who had lined the two sides of the streets were ordered to approach us. The sub-commissioners ordered one soldier to each side of our groups of four prisoners. Four soldiers were at the beginning of the line, and although we did not look back, four others were behind us, surrounding us in a human ring, or more correctly, by a ring of bayonets. It looked as if there were not enough of them. On a new order from the commissioners, the soldiers pulled back and we were ordered to form groups of eight. Naturally, many did not understand what they wanted us to do and a new confusion erupted, until we finally lined up in groups of eight. This took more time. Those of us who had no luggage lined up quickly. But those who were carrying large pieces of luggage on their backs not only moved with difficulty, but also created problems by needing more space around them in the lines.

We imagined the difficulty that people who were obliged to line up with Kechian were experiencing. But he was far from us, in the second or third line, always with that huge package of his bed on his back. We could not see what was happening there.

The sub-commissioners and soldiers, once more, had an opportunity to use force and curse, to push us here and there, until our lines were reorganized. The soldiers surrounded us once more and this time it seemed all was satisfactory, and one of the sub-commissioners gave the orders to move.

"March…"

The orders were directed at the soldiers who started to walk in an orderly fashion. Their heavy jack-boots sounded on the pavement with the nerve racking monotone tic-tac of a clock. And what was left to us was to follow their footsteps. Did we really walk or were we pushed by people behind us, we were not sure.

From that day on, four years of life-in-exile was waiting for me. Exposed to myriads of dangers and deprivations, under a barrage of horrors, often just a few steps from places where, in plain language, Armenians were being slaughtered… I do not remember a more horrific moment than the uncertain time we were walking toward Serayburnu, on the 25th of April 1915, under the silver moon light of that night, in that ill famed alley, surrounded by evil bayonets. I still hear in my head the echo of those contemptuous words directed at us.

I shiver and jump every time I remember that night, although later events, much more evil and tragic, did not affect my nerves in that way. But that night, our drama was just starting, and we did not have experience with danger. We were not mentally equipped to deal with the situation. We were excessively contemplating on things that were not going to happen. Later, owing more to experience than to courage, we did not have the same weakness of deliberating about things that were happening or were going to happen. We remained alert and managed to avoid them.

Up to now I had the opportunity to describe some of our friends, many of whom despaired and saw everything in black. They were unable to shake morbid thoughts of death, and their eyes remained fixed on the ground, as if its muzzle was already open to their uncertain steps. Were these pessimists less courageous than the ones who were joking and laughing? The reactions of the first or the latter were not wilful, but the result of their character. I believe both the contemplators and the ones who kept their humor faced death with dignity, to the extend that such dignity was possible, because many of them were martyred in hideous and torturous ways beyond the human capacity to endure. It is plausible to assume that the pessimists, who were used to the idea of death, remained brave at the ultimate moment, unlike the optimists, who did not believe in death and for whom that outcome was an unforeseeable horror.

That night we did not differ from each other in any way. We were all given to more or less the same black thoughts. I can not remember much from that night journey. I knew that something was happening in this or that line, the number of people who were crying had multiplied, there were people who were sighing, or maybe some people screaming, but I was not cognizant of them. I did not even notice who was walking in front of me, or on either side, or who was in the lines that followed ours. And this state of mind was not particular to me.

The silhouette of Pera, Constantinople, with its familiar terrain and buildings was in front of us, dressed in the sifted silver tones of the moon. We left many sweet memories there, and we could not take away our eyes, or to look at other points. Often we stepped on each other as if we were blindfolded. Many, whose memories we keep in our hearts today, were never to see that view again. We were not going to see many others who were left behind in the suburbs that we could now see on the skyline.

Were those who were left behind crying for us on the skyline? And did others in our ranks, who were in the same mood, direct their gaze to other suburbs of the city? Among us there were people snatched from different corners of Constantinople. In the depth of our inner beings the same emotions were raging and our souls were burning with the fire of nostalgia.

When I finally came to my senses, we were about to leave the Gulhane Rose-alley. Our first lines already passed the border but we were still under the trees. The dense leaves of the trees were covering the skies from our vision. Soldier's regular footsteps, in irritating monotony, could be heard the length of the stone alley. The bayonets on the tips of the rifles were burning like torches under the moon-light. It was a true light festival, and under those cruel circumstances, it felt annoyingly mocking. Perhaps an unpenetrable darkness would have soothed us given our sad voyage.

It was a miracle that the lines that we had formed with such difficulty were kept in order. At least in front of us, as far as we could see, there was no disorder. Yet we did not pay any attention to our steps. It was obvious that we moved forward with the instinctive orderliness of a flock of sheep.

My awakening did not last very long. Once more an inner turmoil gripped me. I could see on my left side the dark waters of the sea, and the reflection of rows of luxurious lights in it. Nothing was floating on its massive surface. It was an embodiment of horror as if a sleeping beast. I recalled the stories told a little earlier, the fear of some, the sighs and the cries of others. The power of these obsessive thoughts was so strong that I could not take my mind off them until, in our turn, we also left the park.

Who thought of this satanic drama? Was there a need for such a large number of policemen and soldiers, and all those terrorizing formalities, which kept us in horrified uncertainty for hours? If they would have informed us that a steam boat was waiting for us in Serayburnu, which would take us to Haydar Pasha [train station on the Asiatic shore of the Bosphorus], and from there we would be taken to a place of exile assigned to us, who was going to argue or show defiance? We had no will power, decisiveness and leadership. Void of all these qualities, we were all puppets, and they could have manipulated us as they wished. Ten policemen would have been plenty to lead our crowd of 199. And truly that was what they had to do that night, take us out of jail and put us on the steam-boat. Had we known this in jail while they were reading our names, the regular rows of the soldiers, even those with the terrifying bayonets, as well as the cruelty and the insults of the sub-commissioners would probably have given rise to sarcasm and perhaps even laughter. In such a case there would not have been horrible stories, the sighs and tears of many people would have been avoided, and we would have passed through that ill-fated road with peaceful heart and light-feet. The road would not have become a source of horror and mental anguish.

Now we could see the steam-boat, which was floating in the lights, in front of the small wharf of Serayburnu. The front lines of our group were close to it and in a short while we were going to be there as well.

Once more there was an unusual abundance of policemen in front of the wharf. Standing beside them were a group of people dressed in civilian clothes. They were surely secret police agents.

An order came to the soldiers surrounding us, while the first among us had reached the front of the wharf. We were to form lines on both sides of the wharf. However, as soon as the soldiers left, in an instant, our lines were mixed up. Some were going forward, others backward to find their friends and acquaintances. One, who came from the front lines told us that the members of the first group who left on the trucks before us were already inside the steamship. Of course he had not seen them all, but he named many with certainty. This circumstance prompted us to rush to the front, as quickly as possible, and soon we were in front of the newest and most luxurious of Shirket-i Khayriye company's steamship, the number 42. When I first saw it, I was moved with memories of so many pleasant trips taken before our arrest.

Chapter 11

On the Steamship

The first news that we got when we boarded the steamship was about the earlier group. Without too much waiting, after being shoved in the trucks, they were brought to the wharf and forced to the steamship under the severest and unnecessary precautions. Of course anxious thoughts and fears had also formed in their hearts, but they were spared the anguish of those horrifying formalities which our group was exposed to. In general they had come with lighter hearts, already aware of being on the road to exile. There was no doubt about that any more. Nobody yet knew anything about the location of exile that we were destined to endure. The names Ayash and Chankiri were equally unknown to us. A few names were circulated with some doubt, such as Konya or Angora. But they were assumptions. Nobody was sure about one or the other.

Those who belonged to the first group told us that the steamship was full of policemen. But from where we stood we could see just a few of them in this or that hallway of the steamship.

Our group dispersed in the steamship without any instruction from the police. If we were left free to our will, we would have taken care of ourselves. Many among us were tired and impatient to find an empty seat. But no one knew how a civilian dressed policeman and his uniformed colleagues attempted to bring order to our group and literally created disorder. They were using such brute force and insults that many retreated rather than going forward.

I succeeded with few friends to make my way to the first class salon. Others before us had done the same thing. When we entered the salon, we saw a few members of our group who had come on foot. Diran Kelegian, Dr. Torkomian, Hayg Khodjasarian and Komitas Vartabed had already found seats. Of course there were others as well, but we had no time to take interest in them. Our attention went to Piuzant Kechian, his bed always on his back. It was a miracle that through all the confusion he was able to make his way to the salon. It was obvious that it had not been easy. As soon as he came in, he dropped the bed on the floor, threw himself on it, took out a huge handkerchief from his pocket, and for a long while wiped it over his forehead, face, beard and neck. Then, taking a long breath, he directed his words to Dr. Daghavarian who was sitting facing him.

"This is the beginning of a long journey, this road has many sweet surprises for us… but where are we heading to?"

The only answer that he received was a forced smile. Daghavarian was not in a good mood although for a moment, when we left the jail, he was not expressing any concern.

Instead of him others replied to Kechian's question. Always the same destinations, Konya or Angora. And guesses started to come from everywhere. Kelegian's fear had taken root in many and they, like him, were scared of being taken to Konya.

Since the yelling and screaming by the police was reaching the salons and did not stop, we went out to find the reason for all the commotion.

A major disorder was reigning everywhere. The police were trying to divide the people in the corridors into small groups in order to occupy different rooms and halls. If they were being unsuccessful, the only thing to blame was their cruelty. The worst among them were the secret policemen, who were cursing indiscriminately left and right. We were not surprised to see Armenian spies among them. This was not surprising given the atmosphere we were in. They did not even attempt to hide their identities from us. The day was certainly theirs.

Krikor Yesayan, who was standing beside me, observed, "These dogs have already counted their chicken. They seem secure in the knowledge that they will never see us again. They are not concerned that at another time, under different circumstances, we will meet them again."

It was a very accurate observation but we did not ponder over it very much.

Gigo, Khachik Idaredjian and Yenovk Shahen had succeeded in remaining side by side. When they saw us far from the crowds in front of the door of the first class salon, they managed to squeeze out and join us.

Exactly at that instant, a secret policeman called the pharmacist Hagop Nargiledjian out of the crowd. The latter, who had been in military service, was dressed in uniform and was led to the lower deck. We thought he was being escorted to one of the special rooms as special respect for his Ottoman military uniform. But the truth was far from our assumption. The policemen took Nargiledjian near the corner of the bathrooms. There they took off the buttons and gold-threaded ribbons indicating his military rank of captain on his uniform, as well as the leather belt off his waist, and then sent him back with an awful curse. This sort of reduction in rank had completely transfigured Nargiledjian, who was not "guilty" and was later one of the first survivor's of Chankiri.

Soon we heard a speeding car stop at the front of the wharf. The car's hooting horn caught our attention. Ibrahim Effendi, the chief of the central jail, and other military personnel came out of the car, and rushed into the steamship without losing any time. They surely went to see the captain. With their arrival the cruelties of their subordinates ended. Not a single curse or threat could be heard. Some of us, who insisted on standing in groups, soon dispersed and found a place either in the salon or in another room. Calm reigned everywhere.

Rosdom Zavarian

At that time Yenovk Shahen, one of those who arrived by truck, told me that Sako had "lost it".

"It started on the road. First he was making incomprehensible groaning noises and repeatedly stating 'Our goose is cooked.' We tried hard to calm him down, but he never responded."

Vramshabuh Samveloff, who had come close to us and was in the same truck beside Sako, confirmed what Shahen had said, adding, "Not only did he not answer us, but he looked at us in a gaze, as if we were all strangers."

Adom Yeritsants had also just joined us. They were on the bridge to enter the steamship. "Sako raised his right arm and, clinching his hand, walked past a group of policemen. One of the policemen noticing it realized what happened and let him pass."

This news caught me by surprise.

"Exile is not a new thing for Sako. He was even in Siberia," I noted.

Sako, whose last name I think was Aghamirzayants, had had a very adventurous life. After the declaration of the Ottoman Constitution, a group of Armenian revolutionaries rushed to Constantinople from different corners and some unspeakable and dark places of the world. He was one of them. He had gained the sympathy and the admiration of all. He was one of the old Hunchagian party members, a man of conviction, who came from a comfortable background but had severed all ties with his family and thrown himself in the activities of the party. He enjoyed the same respect as Simon Zavarian[94] among Tashnag party members; a true patriarch. His physical appearance also remained true to that title. He was of average height, with wide shoulders, and a face surrounded with a huge black beard which covered most of his chest. At the bottom of his wide and smooth forehead, under thick eyebrows, shined his eyes, which expressed more than his mouth. He was taciturn and spoke little. Although he smiled a lot, he was not very friendly. This was surprising in a man who had turned his back on a comfortable life and dedicated his life to the heavy work of the well being of his people. It was difficult to make him join us on happy occasions. There was a big difference between him and the other Hunchag party leader, Sabah-Gulian. The latter liked to *live,* and a half mouthed invitation was enough for him to crash a party with his big family or *ashiret* [tribe] as his friends liked to say. He used to come and take his place at the head of the table, as he was always the self-appointed master of ceremonies.

I did not have much opportunity to see Sako while we were in jail. But on a few occasions when he was in my field of vision, I noticed that there was something missing on him. The events of the day and other conversations and thoughts had not allowed me to reflect on that observation. Now that Shahen, Samveloff and Yeritsants recounted their stories to me, only then I remembered what was missing. Sako did not have his stick with him. He probably did not dare to bring it with him when he was arrested. Calling it a stick is just a way of naming that awesome thing that Sako carried with him. It was a thick piece of curved oak. At the tip, it was shaved to form small and sharp branches. In a strong hand that thing could kill a buffalo with one strike. This stick was an integral part of Sako, some kind of additional limb, from which he was inseparable during his daily life.

When I reentered the first class salon, Komitas had moved from his corner and I do not know how he placed himself between doctors Daghavarian and Torkomian. Both of the doctors were crying. Komitas was looking once at this one and once at the other one with lots of concern in his eyes. We could see him murmuring something to this or that one's ear, probably words of consolation, which we could not hear. We were surrounded by many people from the first group who wanted to know the circumstances under which we were transported to the steamship. We had to repeat ourselves a second or third time to satisfy the curiosity of the ones who joined us anew.

Fortunately the whistle of the steamship put an end to their curiosity. We felt the turning of the wheels and the sound of the water. It was obvious that we were leaving. The police were calling on people standing in the hallways to occupy their place, but this time they were asking very quietly, almost courteously.

Someone informed us that Ibrahim Effendi and the other functionaries did not leave the steamship. Of course their presence had imposed an obligation to behave with courtesy on the part of the police.

Dr. Torkomian got up suddenly and went to the door of the salon and gazed at the moon. After looking at it for a long while, he wiped the tears that were falling on his long beard and forming pearls on his face. He then looked at Pera and mumbled while weeping, "Goodbye... I will not see you again..."

Then he added, referring to his family members, "You, also, I will not see any more..."

And he continued to cry.

They took him and sat him in his place beside Komitas. It seems Komitas had stopped occupying himself with others. He kept his anxious and restless gaze fixed on the floor. We saw Sako, who was sitting on the wood-floor, cross-legged. He was wavering like a devout religious Muslim hodja reading the Koran. He was also oscillating his head as if he was trying to sweep his chest with his long beard.

At times he repeated his theme in a coarse voice, which was difficult to understand, "Our goose is cooked."

Few of his Hunchagian friends, Mourad, Ardzrouni, Stepan Tanielian, Dr. Djelal, and Bedros Kalfayan were beside him, but they did not intervene and waited for him to calm down.

That is the last image I have of him. Sako was the first who lost control, even if it was only for a very short while. Later, we were going to see four others in a temporarily weakened state, the main one being Komitas. He was in an unusually irritated state. He stubbornly insisted on fixing his gaze on Sako, as if he was busy counting the unending movements of Sako's head.

At the second blowing of the horn, the steamship departed from the wharf. Among us there were still people who were given to dark despair. They believed that we could be shot by cannons in Chanak Kale. They were so confused that they did not think that if that was the case, then why would they transport us on the best, newest and most luxurious of the company's steamships, the Number 42? They would have used an old and battered ship.

Mihrtad Haygazn, who had gone out, came in and told us with a smile that we were heading toward Haydar Pasha train station.

That was no news to the majority of us.

Some of us felt a light relief. After all, exile was not a death sentence. Of course there were people who thought that it could be a cause of death, but nobody wanted to disturb the optimism of the moment.

Chapter 12

A Traitor Among the Nobles

When our steamship approached Haydar Pasha station, the vast majority of people threw themselves out of the salon. The ones from the lower deck soon joined us and there was a big crowd on the bridge. A few of the policemen attempted to oppose us and, unable to restrain our curiosity, gave way.

The first thing that attracted our attention was the unusual abundance of lights on the wharf. It was obvious that they were expecting us. Some said that they were going to hand us to the Haydar Pasha police force and pointed to a vast number of policemen who had taken position on the wharf. We could also see other policemen patrolling in pairs.

As soon as the steamship stopped, the director of the central jail, Ibrahim Effendi and his helpers, without paying any attention to us, rushed onto the wharf and went inside the station. We could not take our eyes off him until that point. We could not see everything clearly, but the glitter of the bayonets, to which our eyes had become familiar, was indicative of a major military presence outside. The same show continued here as well.

After a while, when we also came onto the pier, that spectacle revealed itself in a stupefying scene. From the waterfront to the station, on both the left and right sides of the road, were double lines of soldiers. The same thing was on the long stairs to the station. The commanders were not mere sub-commissioners but high-ranking officers.

We were surprised to see such a congregation of military and police forces waiting for us. Surely they could have been more useful somewhere else.

A group of us had hardly landed on the wharf, when the soldiers were ordered to stand guard. The noise of the soldiers' boots striking the pavement filled the air and echoed on the stairs to the station.

"Look at this honor," called out one of us, who had confused this gesture to a salute.

Later in Chankiri, when we were talking about the events of that night, Kechian remembered this moment with a smile.

"I pretended to feel proud when I was passing under the rows of bayonets. Even Kaiser Wilhelm was not bestowed so much honor."

The presence of the military, when we left the jail, or at Haydar Pasha station, and later on the train, as well as on the trip from Angora to Chankiri was unusual. We could have felt more relaxed had we known that, because of a temporary order, the military was given the business of transporting exiled and deported people. We were transported to our destination under military supervision, without understanding the reason for it. On the road we thought that they were just helping the civilian authorities. The truth was completely the opposite. The order for deportations became public 39 days after our departure from Constantinople. We first read about it when we were in Chankiri in "Latest News", which we had acquired by chance. It bore the date of June 2, 1915. When we saw that order, it became clear to us why we were kept under the guard of so many soldiers that night and during the days that followed it.

I tell you in passing that the military authorities did not keep this privilege for long. Soon the job of transporting the exiles was transferred to the civil authorities. *The killings and the massacres started after that.* The date when the order was changed is unknown to me, because it was not published. But I can mention the following. It could give us an idea about a possible date. The last group, which included me, was transported under military control from Chankiri to Angora on Thursday 19 August, 1915. We were more than thirty people. We were transported on military carriages and driven by military coachmen. One soldier accompanied each one of us. Only six among us were the exceptions, Hagop Korian, banker Terlemezian, and others. They were allowed to return to Constantinople. Counting the coachmen as well, we were transported under the surveillance of forty soldiers. Joining us was the best of the policemen of Chankiri, Suleyman, and a gendarme to help him. When we arrived at our first station, at the ill-famed Tuney Khan, Kurd Alo was there with all his *chetes* [irregular soldiers or bandits]. The policeman Suleyman forewarned us not to deal with them. Soon they came to sell us contraband cigarettes. We told them we did not need any. They soon left us alone and left the khan. It is obvious that we avoided a certain massacre because of the presence of the soldiers who were with us.

A week later, on 25 August, another group left Chankiri, among them Taniel Varoujan, Roupen Sevag and three others who shared their fate. They were in the company of a policeman and a gendarme. This time civilian authorities were responsible for their transport. All five of them were killed in front of Tuney Khan by the chetes of Kurd Alo. The policeman and the gendarme were powerless when facing them. One can assume that the transfer of authority from the military to the civilian authorities occurred sometime during the first ten days of August. This transfer had possibly taken

Taniel Varoujan

place in Angora, the seat of the provincial governor, before Chankiri. In any case, after transferring the task of deporting refugees to the civilian authorities, the first caravans of the deported Armenians from Angora were massacred, ten hours from the city, in the valleys of Nenek and Beynam, on August 24, 1915.[95]

Some of the policemen had disembarked the steamship and were on the wharf. A few policemen remained on the steamship and were yelling and making sure that nobody was left hidden on board.

We were walking down the path lined by rows of soldiers in a mixed group. We were all impatient to enter the station and avoid the heavy security that we were surrounded by outside. The group of functionaries had disappeared, who knows to which corner of the station, and the road remained opened to us.

At that time, somebody from the front row yelled, "Long live Armenia." We looked at each other in surprise to see who called out. The news came from mouth to mouth that it was Sako. It was obvious that his nervousness had not dissipated yet. One could hear discontented murmurs rising and people were shaken. But Sako's outcry did not have any effect. The police on the wharf were in the back and were trying to gather people in. They could not hear Sako's outcry from that distance. Even if they heard, no doubt, they were not going to pay any attention to it, assuming that they understood its meaning. In their eyes we were all cut from the same fabric, the kind of people who would cry out "Long live Armenia." The government had condemned us all to exile. They considered all of us enemies of the country. Such an outcry from one or another of us would not have been a surprise to them.

There were many soldiers in the large hall of the station. We were allowed to move around. But the exit doors were all closed, although we did not test them. It was obvious they would have interfered if we tried to open one or the other.

Many of us, who did not have a chance to eat the bread distributed earlier, were completely starving. Those who wisely packaged and carried the bread along with them were surrounded by the starving one's and their bread was plundered in an instant. This pillage became a pass-time for us. Of course, a few people were not amused. But overall it was funny and the soldiers and police started to laugh with us. We were laughing at people who carried the bread with them from the jail to Haydar Pasha but did not manage to put a piece in their mouthes. Many were unfamiliar to us, some of them shady characters from different parts of Constantinople, who brought the bread to sell and make a profit. Kelegian and others explained this to us, and these people were paid more than they expected, which gave rise to even more jokes.

Soon after this incident we learned that a special train was being prepared for us. The guessing started once more. Now everybody was nervous and irritable. There was no doubt about our fate. None of us could accept the injustice of leaving our families and everything dear to us behind and going to an unfamiliar destination.

This irritability led to arguments and insulting comments. The most irritated were the three Kayekdjian brothers, specially the eldest, Mihran. All of them were very conservative people. They had opposed youthful or so-called progressive ideas of the youth in the district of Gedig Pasha. They were called regressive and parochial in the progressive press. Mihran had opened his mouth and was spitting bile at the revolutionaries among us.

"They did what they wanted, they did not listen to us, and look at the result... see our bad luck. We are burning with them."

"And if you would not be burning with them, you would be having a ball," commented someone...

We did not have a chance to hear Kayekdjian's response. A much more serious argument caught our attention. We could see two Hunchag party members,

Haroutiun Djangulian

Haroutiun Djangulian and Ardzrouni (Hagop Avedisian), as well as Smpad Piurad, Gigo, Krikor Yesayan and others, who had surrounded a man whom I did not recognize at all.

I made my way through the crowd and soon learned that his name was Margos Natanian. He was not the well known writer and publicist known to us. He was a lawyer who had lived in Uskudar and then moved to Pera, Ferikeoy, known by the name Margos Natanian. The surprise was not at his wrongful arrest. As I mentioned earlier, the police made many mistakes during hasty and hushed arrests on the night of April 24th. The surprising thing was that this man, who had the gift of the gab, was unable to prevent his transfer from the police station to the central jail. He was screaming out loud that he was a member of Ittihad party and for many years he was a loyal follower of that party. He was an active member of its Pangalti Branch.

The argument, the way we were informed, had first erupted between him and Ardzrouni. Margos informed people surrounding him that he was arrested by mistake and was going to write to Taalat Bey–who was not yet named Pasha–and the general secretary of the Ittihad party, Midhad Shukri Bey, so they could correct the mistake. Of course, this was his right. He also added that he knew Margos Natanian, with whom they confused him, and he knew where he lived. He also knew that the latter was the enemy of the government and was jailed and exiled, where he spent part of his life. He added that to prove his innocence he was going to inform the police of all that he knew, as well the other Margosian's address to prove his point.

Ardzrouni, who was from Van, was of course trying to protect his compatriot and friend from this imminent danger. He pointed out that to protect oneself in such a manner was not very far from betrayal.

"Look at me," the man answered, "by profession I am a lawyer, not a hero. I am not a martyr. I am not interested in self-sacrifice."

This conversation was overheard by Haroutiun Djangulian, who was standing by. He heard the words "hero" and "esh Nahadag" [*lit.* a donkey-martyr]. Djangulian, also a native of Van, was easily irritable and had little control over his words. He delivered harsh words of condemnation addressed at the lawyer and the arguments gradually escalated. Some feared that it could lead to something even worse. Krikor Yesayan was shaking his fists at the men. We pulled him aside, but he managed to yell, "Say it in Turkish, so they can also hear it."

He was referring to the policeman who was standing by without paying any attention to any of this.

"Do you think I am shy to say it?" answered the man.

And he started to groan in a loud Turkish.

"I am not guilty... my name is not Margos Natanian. I am known as Margos Servet... I am not the government's enemy. I am an Ittihadist... the revolutionary is the other one... he teaches Armenian history..."

From Ayash, where he was exiled, he informed the authorities of Margos Natanian's address in a letter pleading for his freedom. The latter was immediately arrested and exiled to Iskilib, near Angora, a Kurdish populated town in the district of Haymana. He would most certainly have been murdered if he hadn't fallen ill. His little daughter wrote a courageous plea to Talaat for the release of her father and was granted it. Others, who were exiled alone in the same region, like Dr. Devlet Dadrian, a member of the National Assembly did not fair as well... although the latter was much less "guilty" of similar things.

The other Margos Servet was allowed to return to Constantinople immediately.

Natanian, God rest his soul in peace, came to visit his sick daughter in Paris in June 1925 and told us the following story. Few years after his return from exile, he was in Ferikeoy. Passing by a church, he heard there was a funeral service. He went to the church to pay his last respects without inquiring into the identity of the dead person. Many did this at the time, using it as an occasion to say prayers for the many martyrs who had perished during the massacres. Only after the service did he inquire about the name of the dead person. The janitor told him that it was Margos Servet who had died.

"I did not regret that I prayed for his soul, and that day I forgave him for the bad thing he did to me."

He thought that this Margos was also from Van. Many families lived in Van, who had the common surname Natanian, but were not related to him.

The entrance of Ibrahim Effendi, the director of the central jail, accompanied by a small group of policemen, put an end to many quarrels and arguments that had erupted here and there. The arguments were going to be restarted on the train later.

As soon as Ibrahim Effendi entered the hall, he advanced to the middle of the crowd. It was obvious that he was going to make an announcement.

Chapter 13

Still in the Dark

Ibrahim Effendi made an announcement that we would be leaving soon. But he did not inform us of the destination or conditions surrounding our travel. He simply mentioned that we would be leaving soon and that all care was taken to assure our comfort.

Later, he added, with a grimace, which was his smile, "Don't worry about anything, I will also join you."

This herald was not a pleasant one for us. Although none of us had seen any ill treatment from him so far, none of us entertained any sympathy or indifference for him. We all loathed him, regardless of the calming effect his presence had on the lesser personnel, or the temporary halt of rudeness and curses from the latter. We probably had a premonition. We knew of the beast that was asleep in him, which was going to be unleashed in full fury in future, during the transportation of the groups of exiles. We now know for a fact that he later turned the Armenian homeland into hell.

As he promised on the road, as long as he accompanied us to Kalejik, our comfort—it is difficult to call it comfort, perhaps we should say our safety—was guaranteed by him. Apart from those instances when we had to make some purchases, he never allowed any Turks to come close to us.

As to the officers, a captain and a few sub-commissioners were in command of soldiers. They always stayed at a distance and never approached us. On the way to exile, whenever we stopped at a station, they immediately ordered the soldiers to stay away from us, in order to prevent any mishaps. It was mainly the policemen and gendarmes who watched us under the all-seeing eyes of Ibrahim Bey.

The latter, after making his announcement, took a sheet of paper from one of the officials who followed him and started to read the names of those who left their money in the depository of the jail. When the person whose name was read out came to the front, Ibrahim Effendi asked him how much money and in which denominations he left it at the depository. Comparing the answer with the list in his hand, he motioned a policeman to return the envelope to the person.

The list of people who left money in the depository was not long. The offer was given to all of us, but without obligation, and only a few among us paid any attention to it. I would like to mention the name of Dr. Hagop Topdjian, who had come to the jail with 100 Ottoman gold coins. He was given back the whole sum. The policemen who returned the money asked him to count it, but Dr. Topdjian, out of consideration not to look rude, declined the offer. I mention this situation just to record the kindness of Dr. Topdjian. In Chankiri, Dr. Topdjian kindly made this money available to his friends and acquaintances. He made personal loans to all who under the pressing conditions of their arrest did not think of bringing money with them. Some of the money he gave to the needy, until monetary assistance came from the Constantinople Patriarchate.

The return of the money that was kept in the depository of the jail was a happy occasion for the owners of the sums, who had already grieved their loss on the way to Haydar Pasha. In general, this development gave rise to optimism, and the faces of many people was lit with hope.

"Because they returned the money, their intention cannot be crooked," observed one person.

Nobody argued that this was only a beginning, and that tomorrow could be different.

Ibrahim Effendi had something else to say. After he finished the distribution of funds, he informed us that he was responsible for the comfort and supervision of our travel. He told us to group together based on our rank or status. He told us that the ones who were of humble means should gather in different groups so that he could make appropriate arrangements in different class wagons. He added that this was not obligatory, but it was preferable to avoid the presence of undesirable neighbors.

These words caused certain snobs with rank and title to come together thinking that they might be given preferential treatment or offered better conditions. But the suggestion of the director of the jail was understood by most as the following: People who had close ties because of special affiliations should gather in separate groups. The revolutionaries, after Ibrahim Effendi and his functionaries left, attempted to come close to each other, Tashnag party members on the one side, Hunchag party members on the other side. There were other groupings around Kelegian and Kechian. Already Dr. Torkomian, the three vartabeds, Dr. Djevahirian, Dr. Nakkashian, Rev. Keropian, the pharmacist Hagop Nargiledjian were close to them and others were heading in that direction. Some were trying to group according to the districts in which they lived. But in general these attempts were not successful. They caused many to complain, others to be sarcastic, and yet others to make fun of some people. The hall of the station was not spacious enough to accommodate such an exercise. Many people were pushed into different corners and were not able to join their friends or people with whom they shared similar outlooks.

When we were invited to board the trains, we were mixed up once more. The only exception were the *ayingadjis* and the undesirables of different streets, who always stuck with each other. They were going to remain like that even at the most crucial moments, when they were taken to be slaughtered.

Outside, on our way to the trains, we passed through two lines of soldiers. There were mostly class B and C wagons waiting for us. The last class B wagon, I suspected, was reserved for Ibrahim Effendi and his functionaries. No one was allowed on that wagon.

As soon as Ibrahim Effendi saw our group, he realized that we did not carry out his recommendation. But he did not show any signs of displeasure. He stood in front of the second wagon surrounded by a few police officers and captains. The presence of the latter was an indication that we would be accompanied by soldiers. When the first person approached him, Ibrahim Effendi politely asked that person to identify himself. Then he pointed to the wagon where the person was assigned, always using the word please. Then the police directed the person to the wagon.

When the approaching person looked well dressed, Ibrahim Effendi would assume an even more respectable attitude when asking about their identity.

"Your honor?"

And the responses were often resounding titles. "The personal physician of his Highness Prince Medjid," "The chief editor of *Sabah* newspaper," "A former Member of Parlament from Sivas," "President of *Mudafaya-i Milli,* Pangalti Branch," "President of the city council of Makri Keoy," "Member of Parliament from Kozan," "The chairman of Kandili Ittihad club," and many others...

Soon this process was over but it did not serve any purpose. After entering the wagon, where there was no surveillance, people went from one wagon to the next to join their friends or people with whom they shared an ideology. Many passed to the C-class wagon, when they were assigned to the B-class and vice versa. People joined their friends and acquaintances rather than following the assignments based on social status. Of course some remained mixed up. Soon the soldiers boarded the wagons, six to each wagon, and their first order of business was to order us not to open windows, not to go out of the wagons, and to remain where we were. Of course they were repeating the orders given to them.

Few orders came from outside, then a whistle blew, and then the noise of the train indicated that we were moving. The train left with a hushing noise.

Our exile had started. We were at Haydar Pasha station for only an hour.

The soldiers took off the bayonets from their rifles and put them away in their jackets. They made themselves comfortable, mostly near windows. They had bad opinion of us. They were told horrible stories about us. They were told that we were arrested for attempting to kill the Sultan or ministers. Regardless of this, they were polite and soon became familiar with us.

Many of us, tired and exhausted from that horrific night's chain of events, fell asleep high with emotions, fears and anxieties. Three of the soldiers in our wagon fell asleep as well. The remaining three remained awake to guard us but soon realized that we were not the dangerous people they were told we were and they also fell asleep.

When, after a short while, I opened my eyes, the wagon had turned into a music hall.

I could only guess the program…

Next Monday morning, on April 25th, we arrived at Nicomedia (Izmit) when it was still dark everywhere. As soon as the train stopped, five of the soldiers rushed to put on their bayonets and left the train. One remained on board as a guard and warned us repeatedly not to open any window.

Although we stayed a while in Nicomedia, we could not get in touch with people outside. Some of us tried to use the bathrooms to look outside, but did not succeed. The soldiers were guarding the hallways and the bathrooms as well.

We were forbidden to move from one wagon to another. However, we were not forbidden to talk. We could pass a word from one end of the wagon to the other by word of mouth. But we had nothing to say to people in our wagon or to people seating beside us.

As soon as we arrived to Nicomedia and the soldiers left the wagon, a word went around that we would be exiled there. Without exception we all believed in this good news and started to happily shout out the news to others. We believed it because the government of the day, after the general mobilization of Turkey, had turned the province of Nicomedia into a place of exile, where the untouchables, such as big gamblers, or dangerous criminals who were convicted three to four times in different regions of Constantinople were exiled.

We did not know the source of the news that had lifted our spirits. Some started to sing. A soldier guarding us was curious to know the reason for our joy. They told him that we would be staying in Nicomedia. Others slipped cigarettes into his palm. It seemed that he also believed the news and weakened his guard. Although we were not able to open a window to glance outside, we were allowed to move around freely from one wagon to the next with a promise to return quickly.

I, with a few of my friends, passed to the next B-class wagon. There was a group of dignitaries in that wagon. Kelegian, Dr. Nakkashian, Rev. Keropian, Ketchian, Dr. Torkomian, Dr. Daghavarian, Arisdages Kasbarian, Dr. Hagop Topdjian, a few senior Tashnag party members, and all of the clergy.

At the moment when we entered, Komitas Vartabed signed a piece of paper which he had in his hand and passed it on to Hovnan Vartabed sitting beside him. The latter also signed and passed it to Balakian Vartabed. I asked Dr. Nakkashian what was being signed?

"It does not relate to us. Of course you heard the news... it seems we will be staying in the province of Nicomedia for a while, until the end of the war... Our clergy is writing a petition to the government to allow them to stay at the monastery of Armash."

The next wagon I entered, I saw Haroutiun Shahrigian, surrounded with the Kayekdjian brothers, who were repeating their usual theme song. It was obvious that the argument, which had started at Haydar Pasha station, was continuing. But the Kayekdjians were in a monologue. Shahrigian did not seem to hear or willing to answer them. There was also Margos Natanian or Margos Servet, who was a natural ally to the Kayekdjians. It looked as if somebody had made an unpleasant comment directed at him and he was yelling

Dr. Hagop Topdjian

"Can't you understand... this is such an affair that the guilty will be punished... and the innocent will be freed... if you are not guilty, make a petition... I am caught instead of somebody else... and I will complain..."

I could not follow the argument any further. At that moment the train whistle blew and started to shake. A few people from the next wagon rushed into ours and said we were moving. Truly, the soldiers who had left the train boarded it again and the whistle blew once more and train was on its way. I hardly had time to run to my wagon, taking with me Dr. Topdjian, who did not want to remain with the famous people. He found their conversation very pessimistic.

When our train started to move toward Bilejik, which we were soon going to leave behind us, the smiles evaporated and gloom took over instead. We were sad because this departure had ruined the dreams that we had just woven in our minds.

The province of Nicomedia was not void of attraction for us. Some of us deceived ourselves by imagining exile as a pleasant pass-time in the countryside. And many among us, including myself, yearned so much to see the most beautiful Bardizag where we held the sweetest of memories.

Chapter 14

A Close Call

Our wagon had the look of a home in mourning when we entered it.
Nobody spoke. Although awake, people kept their eyes shut. This first
disappointment weighted heavily on us. Shoulder to shoulder with Dr.
Topdjian, we closed our eyes and soon fell asleep, having the loud
snoring of a husky soldier sitting across from us in the front row as a
lullaby.

When I opened my eyes the train had already stopped. Other
people had come to us from the neighboring wagons. Ours was the
second after the locomotive, which had stopped just in front of the
train station. Siamanto and Hampartsoum Hampartsoumian were also
in our wagon. Siamanto, with a handkerchief that had lost all claims to
being white, was feverishly cleaning the glass window which had
steamed up and was following the events outside.

I asked where we were.

"Eskishehir," he replied.

There was a tone of anxiety in his voice. I asked what was troubling
him.

"Our fate will be decided here," he replied under his nose.

I was looking at him with surprise.

"Now we will know where they are taking us, Konya or Angora,"
he added while continuing his work.

Truly, the railroad line was divided into two after Eskishehir. One
went to Konya and the other to Angora.

I recalled Kelegian's disgust of Konya, whose governor was Azmi
Bey. No doubt Siamanto also had Kelegian's fear, that no good things
could come from a place where Azmi Bey was the mayor.

Many did not share this fear or found it exaggerated. Krikor
Yesayan, who had moved to our wagon, pointed out the fact that
wherever we went, the governor would be a Turk. And he posed a
question: what was the difference between Azmi or Ahmed, Mehmed
or Musa? Nevertheless, given Siamanto's mood, it was not easy to
convince him otherwise.

The city lights could be seen from the window, quite a distance from the station. Facing us were a row of separate buildings, probably a hotel, a restaurant or a coffee-house, all of which were abundantly lit. Some had the illusion that we would be allowed to spend the night in a hotel. But this stupefying optimism was soon drowned in our laughter.

Neither in the wagons, nor outside, no one took interest in us. The soldiers, who left the wagons, were guarding it once more with their fixed bayonets. One of us said that a captain had ordered the soldiers to keep us under severe surveillance and not to allow us to leave. And he had given them permission to open fire if the order was not followed.

Suddenly Hampartsoumian yelled in his stuttering dialect,

"O...o...o...o... open the windows!"

Others also told us that the windows in the other wagons were all open. We did not know whether the windows were opened by members of our group taking advantage of the absence of the soldiers, thus presenting them a *fait accompli*, or whether they had permission from the soldiers.

When the windows of our wagons opened, everybody naturally rushed to them. There was a big crowd outside. Soldiers, policemen, secret agents were guarding the buildings and the labyrinth created by zig-zaging railroads. For the first time there were no Armenian secret agents, or we did not notice them.

As soon as the windows of the trains were opened a slew of vendors started to move toward the train. The police stopped them. But the resistance did not last very long. Many among us complained that we were hungry. Based on an order, we were allowed to buy food. The main food was *seray burmasi*. It was not very attractive to us. It was heavy on onions and garlic. Our preference went to boiled eggs and olives. The bread in the hands of the urchins was white and delicious, but there were more buyers for the military *tayees*, which were grabbed by all due to their freshness. Some of us asked for tea or coffee. Soon we noted the presence of Armenian vendors. They told us that it was difficult to find coffee. The coffee houses were far. But our wish was going to come true soon, with the help of the employees of the Anatolian Railway Company, which exclusively employed Armenians.[96] They brought us the first cups of tea, but only a few of us enjoyed this service. We were many and it was a long way from the coffee-houses.

These employees, young men, were members of different political parties, the majority from the Tashnag party. When they first approached us, they were dumb struck to learn our names. We learned from them that they were warned that a special train transporting Armenians was coming from Constantinople, but not knowing anything about the mass arrests in Constantinople, they assumed that they were transporting vagabonds. Now they were taken by surprise to see the most famous and elite of the nation, including the chiefs of the Tashnag party among us.

Some of them had acquaintances, friends, even family members among us. They started to look for them, always from outside, as they were not allowed to enter the wagons. They communicated with us through the windows.

They offered us, if we wished, to write letters to Constantinople, stating that they would be happy to take the responsibility for their transport. They offered this service before we even thought about it. We did not know that some of us had already written letters to send to Constantinople at the first opportunity that would present itself. These ready letters were passed on to them with great caution, and they immediately left to hide them in a safe place. Many of us had no paper or pencil. Soon these self-sacrificing young men found what we needed and passed them to us, hiding them in the food packages to avoid arousing suspicion amongst the soldiers. Soon everyone wrote their letters and they were passed on to the railroad employees with utmost caution. This most difficult task was given to the cleverest among us, who were able to do it without being caught under the probing surveillance of many curious eyes.

The only incident that for a moment caused great stress, especially amongst the employees of the railroad, was the carelessness of Nshan Effendi Kalfayan.

This happy go lucky man, after finishing his letter late, forgot the circumstances around him, bent down the window, dangled half of his body out, and extended his letter to the first passing employee. The latter grabbed the letter as fast as he could. But a policeman noticing the occurrence called the worker in a stern voice to see him. The employee, who was carrying a bag of olives in his right hand, panicked and put the olives in his pocket. Kalfayan's letter remained in his left hand.

This confusion was going to save him.

The policeman who had seen how the worker stashed something in his pocket searched his right pocket, only to find a bag of olives, rapped in a piece of paper from an old schoolbook. The policeman passed the paper to a secret police agent standing by, who examined the paper and reassured the policeman that it was an unimportant sheet of paper. The policeman then forgot to examine his left hand, which was holding the letter of Kalfayan Nshan Effendi, and dismissed the railroad worker.

Despite this incident, the railroad workers loitered around us for a while longer under the pretence that they were bringing us food or drinks, while we started to prepare the list of our names to send to the Patriarch in Constantinople. We strongly believed that they were not aware of the arrests of many of us. These lists were prepared in different wagons and only contained the names we could remember as we were not better organized in our effort. The names of the most famous were put on all the lists. Among us there were also people whom we saw in Constantinople jail for the first time. Since we did not take interest in them, we did not know their names. Under the hurried circumstances, when the lists were prepared, there was no possibility to approach people one by one and ask for their names. Those who wrote the lists, after noting the names of the more famous among us, were satisfied by registering our approximate number, which differed from one list to another. At the time we did not know our total number. Some thought we were 200, others more than 200.

We succeeded in passing these lists, without further incident, to the railroad workers. Their self-sacrifice was the first real help that was offered to us since the beginning of our arrests.

This is a good opportunity for me to mention that the self-sacrifice of the Anatolian Railway Company's Armenian employees was to become legendary, a sacred tradition. During the war they bestowed their help generously to all the deportees, aiding many of them during their harsh transport or helping them to escape. Some of them were caught, jailed, and severely punished. After some time, I saw a big group of them in the notorious Sidikli jail of Konya. They were four or five of them, all accused of helping the escape of maximum-security prisoners during their transport.

The government at the beginning of the Armenian atrocities tried many times to clear the Anatolian Railroad's Central Administration and different lines of Armenian employees. Every time they were met by the stubborn resistance of the two general directors of the company, Mr. Huguenin[97] and Mr. Gunther. Both of them were Germans, and they argued against the government's point of view, which was that during the sensitive task of military transports it is dangerous to keep members of a suspected nation on the railway lines. The directors argued that if they did not employ Armenians or Greeks, did the government have competent and experienced Turks to replace them, considering it was the most important quality needed for the job?

Naturally during those days the Anatolian Railroad was crucial for the military forces, and it was impossible to replace the engineers of the railroad from one day to the next, such as M. Maghakian, H. Antreasian and others, or the whole Armenian workforce, where each employee had a responsible job. The government not only had to give in but it also had to accept the demands of Mr. Huguenin and Mr. Gunther to spare the families of the Armenian railroad workers from deportation. Taking advantage of this permission, many of the young Armenian workers married the girls of large and well known local families, thus saving entire families from certain death.

During the entire duration of the war they never stopped helping and providing their assistance and protection to deportees and to individuals under special orders.

We were at Eskishehir train station for more than two hours and we had nothing else to do. We had passed on the last of the letters and lists to the ever decreasing number of railroad workers. Soon one of them informed us that arrangements were being made to send the lists to Constantinople and reassured us that in two days the lists would reach the hands of the Patriarch.

We were impatient to continue and looked in vain for Ibrahim Effendi and the officers accompanying him, whom we had not seen since our arrival at the station.

One more utterance from the stuttering dialect of Hampartsoumian's voice informed us that we were moving.

"We...we... we... will be moving..."

The soldier-guards started to mount the trains, removing the bayonets from their rifles. Soon they ordered us to close the windows.

They all looked tired from standing like statues outside and looked eager to find a corner to slump.

"Where are we going?" I asked one of the hairless soldiers sitting beside me.

"To Angora," he replied under his nose, taking a long yawn, and covering his eyes, without realizing the impact of that name on many of us.

Soon the word passed from mouth to mouth and made the tour of the entire train.

"We are going to Angora," they were sounding from each corner.

People's faces had lit up and joy was radiating from them. Siamanto, who was in our wagon, was pleased and was joking with

Siamanto (Adom Yardjanian)

Hampartsoumian. Since we left the jail, it was the first time that he looked so happy. It was a pleasure to look at him, or to rediscover him. In real life he was a bundle of honey and love.

Echoes of animated conversations were reaching us from the neighboring wagons. It was obvious that the "good" news had left the same impression on all. Some were singing.

Now, after 30 years, I remember the joy that some of us felt during that night.

However, Angora, which was considered a refuge, was soon going to turn into a real hell. For a significant majority of those who rejoiced after hearing of the train's destination, after few months, were going to be killed under the most gruesome and disturbing conditions in this or that corner of that province.

Meanwhile, Konya, which scared so many of us, despite the deportation of local Armenians, would be the safe refuge without as much as a nose-bleed for many thousands of Armenians until the end of the war.

Finally, we also fell asleep like the soldiers. When the train stopped again, the sun had risen and we were at a small station near Angora, Sindjan Keoy, where a bitter surprise was awaiting us.

Chapter 15

Guillotine Drops

When the train stopped at Sindjan Keoy, at first we thought that it was a regular stop. Many of us opened our eyes, remained where we were, and continued to sleep. The soldiers soon left the train in hurry and we heard the sharp voice of Gigo yelling that we had arrived at our place of exile.

All of us hurried to the windows. We could see no building which looked like a station. There was no sign of people. There were a few dilapidated huts, no doubt simply stables. It was obvious that the train had stopped far from a station.

On our right, where the soldiers were, there was a big, bare and uneven space, which formed some kind of square, with a few sparse trees that had sprouted here and there by chance. On the length of that land were rows of freight carts that were used for transportation in Anatolia – *majer arabasi* – all of them with arched covers and without horses. The horses were standing in groups under the trees with their feed bags hanging down their necks.

Those freight carts were going to transport us, and we imagined the torture on the stony, rough and rugged, usually half ruined roads of Anatolia. In day to day life people spread beds and stuffed pillows on the sides of the carts to cope with the torture resulting from the gyrations of the road. We did not even have an extra handkerchief on us, let alone beds and pillows. The soldiers had fixed their bayonets once more on their rifles and were guarding both sides of the train, especially the right side, where the freight carts were. A few of the coachmen were outside and others were coming out of the huts at the orders that were yelled like the cracking of whips by the sub-commissioners surrounding their captain, or from the orders of policemen or gendarmes spread out at different points.

The carts were saddled in a great hurry. They had not given us any orders, but it was obvious that we were going to be ordered out of the train pretty soon. We toured the other wagons to see if we could gather any information, but nobody had any news of the intention of the people who were leading us. There was no doubt, after seeing the freight carts being saddled, that we were going to be sent quite far from the railroad tracks, but where to? That was still a complete mystery for us.

We do not know from where Ibrahim Effendi appeared, but he quickly moved toward the captain, surrounded by a group of officers. After a short exchange, during which he did most of the talking, Ibrahim Effendi, while holding a piece of paper, called over one of the policemen and rushed him to the coachmen with instruction to make them hurry. They were not standing idle. The vast majority of the freight carts were ready and waiting in a row, one behind the other.

Sarkis Minasian

Following the order of Ibrahim Effendi, a policeman approached the train in hurried steps. We could not see but we gathered that he was coming on board, and we rushed to the door of our wagon to pass to the next wagon. There was no need for this. People started to pass on the message.

"Open the windows looking on to the freight carts!"

The policeman who had given this order continued, "Those whose name is called must come out immediately."

Then he left.

Although the windows of our wagons were opened very quickly, those of us in the back could not see anything. People at the front squeezed near the windows and covered our vision. Our curiosity was so great that we were pushing each other and squabbles broke out for a moment, until people occupying the front line yielded a little.

A voice from outside repeated the order.

"Whoever hears their name, should come out instantly, bringing their bags with them."

"*Soos, soos* [quiet, quiet]!" people were sounding from everywhere, concerned that during this havoc, they could miss what was said.

Soon after we heard the first name, which was that of Kris Ricci. Then we heard those of Agnouni, Khajag, Shahrigian, Roupen Zartarian, Sarkis Minasian and others in the same order that we were called when we were leaving the jail. Ibrahim Effendi was reading the same list as was done by the spy Hidayet, I suspect with difficulty, because many names they could not pronounce correctly, but we understood whom they were referring to.

Gradually the following people left our train, Yenovk Shahen, Siamanto, Hampartsoum Hampartsoumian, Kegham Parseghian, Partogh Zorian, Levon Shamdanjian, a young fellow from Uskudar who was arrested by mistake instead of Mikayel Shamdandjian, and other unknown people whose names we had never heard before. With the departure of this group of people, a place opened near the windows, and we all moved to the front row. We could now follow the events outside without hindrance while Ibrahim Effendi continued his lecture of the names.

Kegham Parseghian

The policemen were constantly around Ibrahim Effendi. The military men surrounded him, and nobody was paying attention to the people coming out of the train. The latter had grouped around the freight carts following their personal affiliations, Tashnag party members were on one side, Hunchag party members on another, those who did not belong to any party yet at a different place. Kris was alone, leaning on a tree and, as usual, careless. He was smiling at us from a distance, as if to say not to worry. There were also those who remained truly confused like the butcher of our street, the dog collector Asadourian, and others who were unfamiliar to us. They were truly harmless people who had no idea what was going on. They were especially confused how they were related to the others in the group, whose names they might have heard before, but with whom they never had any relations. There was no doubt that many of them they saw for the first time, and they were wondering at the silly joke of fate that placed them in the company of these famous people under such worrisome circumstances.

Behind the policemen were a few curious Turks who had gathered around, wicked faced people, who remained at a distance in front of those semi-ruined huts. They were seemingly instructed to remain where they were. Ibrahim Effendi, who still continued to read from the list in his hand, suddenly yelled, "Hayit [Hayg] Tiryakian…"

A man of advanced age, with one swollen eye, his right leg in bandages, came off the train with the aid of a cane and silently approached the policeman.

Mikayel Shamdandjian

Exactly at that same time from another wagon flew out the editor of *Azadamard* publishing house, the Tashnag party member Hayg Tiryakian (Hrach). A few of the policemen ran to the latter and yelled,

"*Icheri… icheri* [In… in]!"

Tiryakian did not pay attention to their screams and kept on moving forward, until the policemen held him by force. Ibrahim Effendi, who had stopped his reading, saw what happened and ordered him to be taken back to the wagon. But Tiryakian was complaining that his name was read.

"I am Hayg Tiryakian," he screamed, "Ask all my friends who have already been called. There they are!"

And he pointed to the huge group of Tashnag party members.

While they had stopped him, the other Tiryakian, the old one who was limping, arrived near Ibrahim Effendi and the people surrounded him.

A policeman asked him for his name.

"Hayg Tiryakian," the old man answered.

"Go and stand there," said Ibrahim Effendi, pointing to the ones already standing in a mixed group.

Then turning to the policemen holding the real Tiryakian, he ordered, "Take him to the wagon."

His order was soon carried out, despite Tiryakian's loud protestations.

This way, the elder person, who was most probably arrested by mistake, was taken out of his bed and driven up to this point, in his sick state, half blind and hardly able to move. He remained with the Ayash prisoners. People who knew him said that he was one of the owners of the Minerva grocers on Pera avenue.

The real Tiryakian, Hrach of Trebizon, was well known to the police. It is enough to say that he was one of the Tashnag party terrorist members who had occupied the Ottoman bank in Constantinople on 13 August 1896.[98] He was freed with the entire group of his friends, because of the intervention of foreign embassies. After leaving the country for a while he returned under cover to Izmir as a party agent. He was arrested and was condemned to life imprisonment and exiled in Bodrum, from where he was freed on the eve of the declaration of the Ottoman Constitution [in 1908]. He was also known in government circles not only as a famous Tashnag party member and the manager of *Azadamard* printing house, but mainly as the president of a commercial company which supplied materials to the ministry of war.

Tiryakian never stopped complaining in Chankiri, where he was exiled with us, magnanimously pointing to the mistake of the police, demanding the freedom of the elderly grocer, and his own transfer to Ayash alongside his friends.

"This is a big burden on my conscience," he said repeatedly, referring to the man who was arrested by mistake in his place.

Finally they satisfied him by freeing the old man who was allowed to return to Constantinople. Tiryakian, as per his wish, was transferred to Ayash, and after a short while, on 18 August 1915, was one of the last ones to be killed.

Ibrahim Effendi soon finished reading the list and all who were called came off the train. They numbered 71, the same as in the jail.

We thought that next it would be the turn of those who remained on the train. But Ibrahim Effendi, who had passed the list that he read to the policemen, did not have another paper in his hand. We did not want to believe that they were separating us into two groups. While we were thinking about this separation, a few of the men who had left the train approached the wagons and brought us some news which they had gathered from the coachmen. The first was that the place of exile assigned to them was Ayash, and that we were going to continue our way until Angora, which was an hour and a half away from Sindjan Keoy.

At that moment we were more interested in them than ourselves. We asked what kind of a place was this place called Ayash. Someone answered that it was a small town near Beypazar, populated purely by Turks. That was the first time we had heard of that name which was later going to be so tragically familiar. We did not know much about Beypazar, but at least it was familiar to us by its delicious melons, as much as the similarly unforgettable honeydew melon of *top atan* of Izmir.

Then others approached us. Handicapped, Onnig from Rodosto, the tenant of the Armenian coffee house in Pangalti, a seasoned revolutionary for whom jail and the exile were not unfamiliar, commented, "I don't like what's going on," as he shook his head right and left.

This separation did not look good to many of us. Some had dark thoughts. Others expressed their distress by gesturing with their hands or head.

Roupen Zartarian had leaned on one of the freight coaches, his hands in his pockets, his shoulders stuck out, his collar up around his neck, his face pale, and his gaze fixed on the floor. It was obvious he was still sick. He was shivering like all of us. It was a very cold morning. But in his case, it portrayed his distressed psychological anguish. From the first moment of his arrest, he had a premonition that his end would be tragic. At that moment he did not see death very far. Khajag was beside him and murmuring something in his ear. He was probably trying to comfort him.

Kegham Parseghian was also distraught like him. We could see clearly his distressed look a few steps away with a group of friends his age. Gigo, who was in the group with them, whom we had seen in unsettled mood since his arrest, at times happy and at others sad, was now transformed, yelling out to us with a big smile, "See you when things change…"

Others, who were not obsessed with the ideas of death, were expressing their hopes and desire of reunion in different ways.

Dr. Daghavarian was also surprisingly transformed. He had cried abundantly in the steamboat. Now he looked relaxed and was conversing with people around him.

Smpad Piurad, whom we often saw worried in the jail and on the road, now looked careless and was joking and giggling loudly with people around him.

But the funniest take came from Mihrtad Haygazn. A man with a gift of easy communication, he was able to befriend the coachmen and gathered information from them which he immediately passed on to us.

"We are going someplace really affordable!" he yelled, "An *okha* [oke] of meat is three ghurush, butter seven, chicken two, and ten eggs for one ghurush…"

One has to imagine the degree of his light heartedness. Even those who were heavily weighted down and perplexed with dark thoughts of life and death began to laugh.

Ibrahim Effendi, who after reading the lists had continued to converse with the police officers, left and boarded the first wagon allocated to him. He was followed by the captain and a few of the sub-commissioners. The policemen were busy loading our friends.

The carts started to move. In each cart there were four of our friends. They were loading haphazardly or by police instructions.

The soldiers started to board the wagons and took off the bayonets from their rifles. Some remained behind to board the carts that were still there.

A police officer shouted an order.

"Close the windows."

The order did not cause any displeasure. It was getting colder, and the temperature had started to bite us.

I looked out for the last time. Many were already in the carts and had disappeared under its covers. Few were still outside, surrounded by soldiers and policemen. The last faces that I noticed were of Parsegh Shahbazian, the old grocer by the name of Hayg Tiryakian, and Dr. Nakkashian, who were boarding the cart. Two policemen were helping the grocer because he was having difficulty boarding on his own. And Nakkashian had his arms on the shoulder of Shahbaz, most probably murmuring supportive remarks. Shahbaz was crying…

The windows were already closed. We sat on the benches sad and exhausted. The separation from the group that was heading to Ayash left us demoralized. We had no clue about the implication of this development. Many of the people who were separated from us were dear friends with whom we had spent intimate moments from the beginning of this ordeal, whose absence we were going to feel bitterly.

Somebody murmured on my side, "The bastards chose the crème de la crème among us to put down."

I was not curious to know who made that comment as I was given exactly to the same thoughts.

When our train hit the road, the carts carrying the others were still on the square.

Chapter 16

The Butcher of Ankara

Our train was dashing forward through borderless, treeless, and stony fields. There were odd trees here and there in mostly barren lands, and tombs of wild dusty and thorny bushes covered by piles of earth. But further from them, near the horizon, there were unlimited fields of different hues of green, red and lilac, like colorful carpets under the rays of the sun. Sometimes, in the distant horizon, smoke would be coming out of chimneys, and this told us of the presence of villages, which appeared and disappeared on the horizon.

None of us was in a conversational mood. We were thinking about the unexpected separation that took place in front of Sindjan Keoy. We could not explain the reason but we all felt the pain in our chests. Our minds could not accept the cruel truth that we were separated from our beloved friends forever. The soldiers, who felt more familiar to us, were more talkative. They even allowed us to open our windows when the smoke of our never-ending cigarettes was about to choke us.

It seemed that the soldiers were from this region. Once in a while one of them broke the silence by yelling, *"Ishde bizim keoy"* [There you have it, our village], and he pointed to a direction, which we ignored, and he called out the name, which we instantly forgot.

There was no doubt that they were all village boys. Their eyes were fixed on the productive fields, until the hills covered their view. The tenderness and the eager reappeared in their eyes once more when the train passed those hurdles and the horizon was cleared and the fields reappeared even in more mesmerizing colors. But soon they were overtaken by a sad thought. They had sown the fields but who was going to harvest them? The men were all conscripted for jihad, because of the bloodthirsty leaders who were at the helm of the government's criminal policies.

Varoujan [the famous Armenian writer], who had remained in our wagon, could not take his gaze off the borderless green fields. The fields, after covering the land, had dressed the distant dwarf hills with ceremonial toga, as if a string of beads covering Angora from our vision. Was the ill fated poet experiencing an inspiration in what he saw, which was going to be written later in Chankiri? His last works were dedicated to the glory of the land, the angst lived by the peasants, and the abundance of the harvest during the lucky years. Referring to what he saw, he said, "I will write a *'cultivator's piece'* "

One of us asked a soldier sitting beside him if there was anyone from Ayash among them. He answered that there was none, but he added that he knew Ayash very well. Of course we immediately showed great interest and wanted to know about Ayash. The soldier described it as a town built in a valley nestled between two mountains, where the weather was pleasant even during storms because of the north and south mountain ranges protecting it.

We questioned if there were buildings to house our friends.

"But they are not going to the town," the soldier clarified himself.

"Then, where did they go?"

"They went to the *gheshla* [garrison]," he added with a surprised tone because we did not know.

Then he said that the garrison was built quite far from Ayash, at the foothills of a cemetery, and our friends were going to stay there.

"Tonight they will be there," he added.

We were half reassured for them, but the word garrison left a bad impression on us. At that moment we did not know that the same luck was going to befall us somewhere else. We thought that a garrison was another kind of jail, devoid of the advantages of a real jail, which could be made comparably tolerable by greedy guards.

We had no time to pose further questions. An order from the neighboring wagon had rushed the soldiers to their feet and they got ready to leave the train.

"We have arrived at Angora," our friends called out from the same wagon.

Indeed, the train stopped after a short while at Angora station, which was at the outskirt of town. Approximately two hours had passed from the time we had left Sindjan Keoy.

Following the soldiers, we also left the train, initially with hesitation, but then with more courage. No order was issued but almost all of us were convinced that we would be exiled in Angora. We were impatient to learn about the conditions of our exile. Nobody said anything and this fact further convinced us of the truth of our assumption.

Soon we noticed that on both sides, on the left and on the right, a large crowd of policemen surrounded the train. This crowd swelled even more when the policemen who had secretly traveled with us also joined them.

The only road that was not blocked by the security people was to the huge courtyard of the train station. Already many of us had taken that direction.

The city, spread like a crescent on a vast elevation, was sitting and facing us. From where we stood, we could not see her well. What we could see was an unattractive clutter of uneven and ugly buildings, as if piled up on each other as a pile of stone rubble. The Turks possessed the art of disrupting the natural harmony and beauty of historic vistas under their rule. After Constantinople, Angora was one such masterpiece of their unmatched talent.

Soon, our eyes, disgusted with that ugly scene, rested on a beautiful valley, naked but well flattened, leading to a vast meadow, surrounded by gardens and thick rows of plush trees. There was an abundance of the same green on small hills whose tops could be seen behind it.

"Those are the orchards," said one of us, who seemed to be familiar with the city.

The same person or somebody else added that all of it belonged to Armenians.

Beautiful summer residences could be seen through the trees and gardens. Confident that we would remain in Angora, we gave in to stupid dreams. A month or two sojourn in one or another of those summer-houses was such a sweet dream that we were unable to shake free of the thought. Later, when we were on treacherous and endless roads, we were going to dream of places with hardly had any appeal, but they too were not going to materialize.

We moved toward the courtyard of the train station, where our friends were making lots of noise. Each and every one of us had something to say. Nobody had any desire to listen. In general, most were assumptions on the fate that was awaiting us. Some of us had made the rounds around the station. The security was lax, to be more accurate, non-existent. The soldiers had disappeared and the policemen kept the chain they had formed on our left and right side but remained at a distance from us.

The news from those who ventured out was that policemen were guarding behind the station. A few managed to buy some food. This encouraged others to also go out to buy food. They had seen carriages and horses being saddled on the right side of the station. This worried some of us who suspected that we would be boarding them to be taken to an unknown destination, as was the case in front of Sindjan Keoy. This worry did not spread. We still firmly believed that we were staying in Angora. After all, the presence of carriages near a train station was normal. Even if the carriages were for us, we thought that the station was far from the city, and we did not know which quarter we would occupy.

The noise immediately stopped upon the appearance of Ibrahim Effendi. The director of the central jail, surrounded by his usual entourage, cut through our crowd and advanced to the end of the courtyard. The policemen took a stand on both sides of the two doors leading to the class A and class B waiting halls. Ibrahim Effendi tried once more to divide us into two, leading the famous among us to the A-class and the leftovers free to arrange themselves in the B-class salon. He was becoming familiar with a few of the former people and always showed the utmost courtesy. Using referential gestures he invited them near him and directed the policemen to lead them to the A-class salon.

People who enjoyed that preferential treatment moved forward with special body gestures to attract his attention and make his job easier. Others, even more impatient, loudly announced their social status. All of them went to the first class salon. With them, also went a few practical jokers. Krikor Yesayan presented himself as a forest controller, I do not remember for which area. Someone else, Mugrdich Barsamian, a humble arms merchant, became a supplier for the military. They were hardly able to hold their laughter, seeing how the policemen were leading them with such respectful hurry to the hall.

This process took a long time. As before, the exercise proved to be useless. As soon as Ibrahim Effendi left, people went to their preferred halls.

In the first hall I went, some people had already asked the policemen why we were still waiting. The policemen told them that a high ranking official was going to announce the arrangements that were made for us. Soon we found out that that person was Behaeddin

Bey, the chief of Angora police. This news disturbed us for a while. We would have preferred a municipal official addressing us. The name of the police always bore an ominous sign, and the name of this chief was not going to change that impression. But we concluded that we were prisoners after all and wherever we went we would be dealing with the police.

We speculated on possible restrictions imposed on us in exile, but none of us was certain of anything. The "specialists" Mihrtad Haygazn, Mourad, Djangulian, Sako, Smpad Piurad and others were all left in Sindjan Keoy, and our opinions were all speculative and lent themselves more to jokes than to any conclusions.

Soon we heard the policemen warning each other about the arrival of the chief. They moved and lined up in two rows near the door. All of us, with understandable curiosity, fixed our gaze on the door. The door opened wide and a handsome, tall, well-dressed young man walked in, followed by a few civilian officials, a police commissioner, and three or four policemen.

That was the chief of police for Angora, Behaeddin Bey. At that time he was an unknown functionary who was soon going to earn a sad reputation by playing a major role in organizing the mass murder of Armenians in the city and surrounding large Armenian communities.

Eventually he was going to lose his post and summoned to Constantinople in front of the court, not for killing Armenians after deporting them, but for confiscating their wealth in exaggerated scandalous ways...

Chapter 17

Lablabiji Hor-Hor Agha.
Familiar in the Sea of Horror

Behaeddin Bey was gleaming with a smile when he walked through the rows of policemen and came to the middle of the hall. He stopped and asked loudly, "Where is Kelegian Effendi?"

The question was so unexpected and sudden that we did not pay attention whether it was directed to us or the policemen.

Some of us had the illusion that he was called to be released and return back to Constantinople.

Kelegian was not very far and approached him.

Behaeddin Bey introduced himself, half curving his tall and fine body, always with a smile on his face.

"Bendeniz...Enkara Vilayeti polis muduri" [Your servant... The chief of the police of Angora province].

Ah, when those educated Turks wear the mask of refined manners... If only one could have read his true thoughts at that moment when he uttered with most humility the caressing word *"Bendeniz"* [Yours]. It felt more venomous than a curse word. As much as we did not know him, we had the impression that he simply was making fun of Kelegian.

But he played his role very well. Turks excelled in this domain. They mastered this art. Their policies were based on this kind of deception and always succeeded and continue to succeed.

Behaeddin Bey acted like a host who was surprised by an important dignitary's visit to his house. Kelegian, after the initial shock, or more correctly, a minute of surprise, carefully listened to the cunning flattery of the chief of police who was singing his praise as a teacher and a publisher.

Later, Kelegian admitted that for a moment he hoped that after that barrage of pompous eloquence he would be given news of his release.

"But," he added, "the thought was as fast as lightning and did not linger for long. Although I did not believe that he was sincere, I had a moment of satisfaction that a word was being directed at us, some kind of an explanation being delivered, which had not happened since our arrest."

But Behaeddin Bey did not give any explanation. He continued to use the same sweet language and addressed his words to Kelegian.

"I regret that we meet in these circumstances... but we have no say in the matter... These are, as you are aware, *siyasi ishler* [political matters] related to government decisions. It is above and beyond our comprehension..."

With this speech, he made it clear that we could not expect any explanation from him about our exile.

He continued for a while with vague words and expressions, which in no way helped us clear the dark thoughts in our heads.

Kelegian, in turn, thanked him with a smiling face. He spoke in a familiar tone, carefully choosing his words not to betray his inner worries and anxieties to this minor official. He spoke like a man who accepted his fate which had been decided and implemented by the big beasts in Constantinople. He did not want to show imprudence by expecting anything from this secondary official.

Some found the respect given to Kelegian very appealing and gradually approached the police chief, hoping to catch some of the sweet-like-honey-fireworks oozing out of his words.

But Behaeddin Bey did not address other individuals and directed his words to all of us.

"I reassure you that you have nothing to worry about... The Minister Bey (alluding to Talaat Bey) issued special orders to the governor to spare no efforts to assure your comfort... Unfortunately you have arrived early and he could not receive you personally... If he would be here, he would repeat the same words to you... You are going to stay for a while until the storm has passed... this is all that is happening... special officials will accompany you to satisfy all your legitimate requests so you remain comfortable... do not worry... it is nothing... it will pass..."

These were only words which did not bring clarity to our minds. However, he did reveal one thing which we already suspected: by saying "until the storm has passed", he let us know that we would be in exile until the end of the war, or until there was a change in the mood of the government. But this was not unknown to us. We were already experiencing it. What was burning in us was the reasons for such treatment. The heterogeneity of our group was confusing to us. In our big crowd, the exiled people did not fall into the same category, they did not belong to any special social group, special activities, or convictions. Earlier I had a chance to tell you that some of the people were opposed to each other, and they were even fighting each other. If there was an element among us who was against the government and the Ittihad party, there was also a faction that more or less had corroborated with it.

As to the "stories" that we were told regarding the caring concerns of Talaat and the special orders to the police to take care of our needs, I do not believe that any one of us was stupid enough to buy that nonsense.

It was obvious that Behaeddin Bey was making fun of us as he had done with Kelegian. But we listened to him with great curiosity. We listened to him with the attention of a people who were burdened with a premonition of something dreadful approaching. But we were willing to listen to any reassuring words, knowing too well that those words were far from any truth and only meant to calm our fears. If Behaeddin Bey would speak for hours, we would have listen to him with the same interest.

But he ran out of things to say. He seemed to have more on his mind, but he was looking for ways to say it. Dr. Miskdjian came to his aid unknowingly.

We still believed that we would be exiled in Angora. Behaeddin Bey had not said anything to dismiss that belief. Dr. Miskdjian, who had the same belief, asked if he could stay with his relatives in Angora.

"You are not going to stay here for long," Behaeddin Bey answered. "If there was time, we could have asked them to come and see you here... but you will be leaving soon."

"We will leave?"

Many people posed the same question at once.

Behaeddin Bey continued.

"To tell you honestly and regretfully, there are certain orders. For your sake, it is best that you leave at once... The carts are ready and there will be bread distributed so you have no discomfort on the way."

"But, where are we going?" asked Dr. Miskdjian in a hardly audible voice.

"Chankiri."

This name passed from mouth to mouth, not only in our hall but also to our friends who were in the B-class hall and were not aware of what was happening in this hall.

Behaeddin Bey then added, "It is only a three day journey, that is all... it is nothing... it is nothing..."

Those were his last words. After exchanging a few words with the police, he went back to the door of the salon through the corridor lined up by the police. As he was entering the room, Apig Djambaz pushed his way through the crowd and, almost out of breath, approached him for permission to speak with him.

The police chief had no intention to listen to any requests.

"I told you all that I had to say. I have nothing to add."

But Djambaz was a stubborn man. He repeated his theme song once more. We had lost count of how many times since his arrest he had repeated the same thing, "But Bey Effendi, I was brought here by mistake... I am not Armenian, nor a member of any committee. I am Catholic..."

He wanted to say more, but Behaeddin Bey cut him short and informed him that he did not have the legal authority to correct a mistake that took place in Constantinople.

"When you arrive to Chankiri, you can write a petition to the Minister Bey and you can inform him the things that you told me."

And he disappeared in a split second.

The bewildered old man was left asking, "What is going on...? Where are we going from here...?"

He was made to understand that we were going to Chankiri, and we might stay there until the end of the war.

"Mother of God, St. Maryam," he murmured under his nose...

But we had no time for him. The police had become restless. Everything was ready and they wanted us to move. Now that we knew our destination, we wanted to inform our families and friends about it. We had bought some post cards and were trying to write our notes or telegrams which had to be in Turkish. Some of us were waiting so others could help them.

But soon police impatience took another tone. They formed a ring and started to close in on us so that we would leave the hall. Only a few were able to drop their cards in the nearby corridor where the post box was located. The remainder of the cards were left in our hands. A

Turkish railroad worker accepted the offer presented to him by Mikayel Shamdandjian to post the cards and the telegrams for us. People paid him handsomely for the cards and the telegrams, adding a handsome tip to the count of words. The man left with a nice sum in his pocket. Once in Chankiri we were able to keep constant contact with Constantinople. We soon learned that none of the telegrams were sent, only the cards which did not need additional postage to be mailed.

We had no reason to drag our feet any more. We arrived at the door of the station, passing through unending rows of police. We were under serious surveillance. They were scared that some of us would try to escape to the city. No one had any intention of running away. We all felt lighter, less worried, once we knew our destination. Although we did not know much about Chankiri, the place which was going to be our unexpected place of residence, the name was familiar to us and the Turkish population of the town had a good reputation. Although stubborn and old fashioned, they were supposed to be good hearted and approachable. They were known as *leblebiji,* [roasted chich pea makers] and for their skills as bargemen of Sharab Iskelesi. In comparison, we did not know much about Angora. It was a big city, full of police and secret agents, and a police chief whose acquaintance we had the pleasure to make, a man who did not leave a very reassuring impression. No doubt if we were left in Angora, the surveillance would have been much stricter than in Chankiri, which was just a little quaint provincial town.

Many among us seemed to share these feelings. As we went close to the station door, despite the prevailing confusion, we could hear the humming of familiar tunes from the operetta by Dikran A. Chukhajian, *Leblebiji horhor agha.*

Some in our group were giggling, which was causing annoyance to the "distinguished" men among us.

Komitas was also among the "distinguished group." Following him was Piuzant Kechian, whose huge bed was covering Komitas from our sight. Once in a while Komitas stuck his head out of the corner of Kechian's huge bed and, looking at the singers, gave his tacit approval with a warm smile. Then, as if to avoid irritating the already annoyed ones, he looked away to hide his smile. He looked adorable. His smile was like a song to us.

Chapter 18

160 km Joy Ride!!!

As we left the station and headed toward the square, we walked in a generally good mood through the corridor created by the police. On that Tuesday of 27 April 1915, a bright sun pleasantly warmed us. Parts of the songs from *Leblebiji,* also mumbles of some Turkish folk songs, could be heard from here and there. A loud voice from the front row brought the news that they were distributing bread and this ended all the singing. We could smell the tantalizing aroma of the freshly baked bread and our mouths were watering with anticipation of having that fresh out of the oven dough which had been baked to crispy perfection. It had been 15 hours since we had anything to eat.

The two sack-cloth bread bags were half empty when we approached them. The bread was being distributed by municipal officials under the supervision of a few policemen. The distributed bread was the famed large white bread of Angora. Despite our hunger we did not extend our hands eagerly. The distribution of the bread, as it had in the central jail, reinforced the cruel idea that we were under arrest and were prisoners. We had forgotten it for a short while after discovering our destination. But the sadness that took hold of us abated like a flash of lightning after we took the bread.

The square where we headed looked as if it was under construction. There were piles of stone and earth, bags of sand, wooden structures to mix the cement. People felt free to use it as toilets, and piles of excrement and puddles of urine filled the uneven surface of the ground. It seemed that the animals also had access to the square. There were traces left by them as well all over the place. And all of these sights were in the square of rich and important Angora's railroad station.

The policemen who had closed access to the left side and front of the square, were obviously annoyed at the awful stink that was in the air and wanted us to hurry by pointing to an elevation on the right side, where we saw Ibrahim Effendi standing surrounded by policemen and gendarmes. But there was no need for instructions. We were as annoyed and rushed without coercion.

The height which we climbed dominated over a vast area which was not obvious from the square. It was a suburb of the city full of greenery. The first who arrived had already boarded the coaches. Surely there were many more coaches before our arrival. There was a vast group of soldiers standing around without orders in a relaxed manner. Soon we descended to join our friends. Only after the last among us descended, Ibrahim Effendi and the soldiers and gendarmes also descended.

All the coaches were ready for departures. They were mostly *majir arabasi*s with dirty and discolored covers. There were coaches with six suspensions, relatively comfortable

Krikoris Vartabed Balakian

*yayli*s, one of which was standing apart. No doubt it was reserved for the officials travelling with us.

Once more, Ibrahim Effendi tried to separate us into classes, by choosing those with whom he had become familiar to ride in the *yayli*s. He behaved courteously as always with chivalrously words in his mouth. The first among them were Diran Kelegian. Dr. Torkomian and Rev. Keropian. In another coach Balakian and Garabedian Vartabeds. I am not sure if Komitas was with this latter group, but in any case he was one of the privileged. With him was also Hagop Korian and Father Housig, both of them advanced in age, who required help of the others to mount the *yayli*s.

At least this time Ibrahim Effendi could be sure that we were not going to disturb the order that he created. It was impossible to move from one coach to the other. But his efforts were once more going to remain fruitless. Soon the five *yayli*s available were filled, three people per carriage, and the less famous had to look for places in the common coaches.

Each of these coaches was designated for three people. The policemen were issuing instructions in this regard, for people to move in this and that corner. Some of us just mounted on any available coach. Others tried to stay with friends and acquaintances. Each time one of us mounted the coach a scream of discontent could be heard. It was difficult to find a comfortable position in those accursed torture chambers covered by wooden planks.

Kechian was going to be rewarded for the torture of carrying that heavy weight with him throughout the journey. It was his right of course. He had spread his mattress and the cover on the floor of the coach and was kneeling to arrange the pillow to support his back from the jolts of the road. I do not remember the names of the other lucky ones who shared his coach. Most probably one of them was Dr. Djevahirian, his brother in law, who remained with him like a shadow. They were going to be the ones to travel in the most comfort, including the soldier assigned as a guard in their coach. A second soldier was installed near the coachman. The bayonets were exposed on the rifles of each of the soldiers. This was the case for the *yaylis* as well.

Der Vartan Karageozian, the father of Ferikeoy, Hayg Khodjasarian and I were allotted a frail coach, with semi wet floors. We tried to lie down as a trial, to see if we could be comfortable, but we had no time. A stout soldier climbed the coach and sat down near the edge by folding his legs. He looked so comfortable, as if he was sitting on a cushion. Hopeless, and following his example, we also folded our legs, which we could not extend anymore. I just could not imagine for how long we could remain in that position.

We could hear more and more discontented voices all around us. Even some swear words were being heard. One of the last men who climbed a neighboring coach was explaining to a friend in a loud voice that he glanced at a map in the railroad station, and added jokingly.

"It is not much really, a mere 160 km!!!"

We could not hear the answer, but a curse word would not have been surprising.

We had a short intermission with the surprise appearance of vendors. The policemen were encouraging us to take advantage of them and to buy food. They informed us that the road ahead was long and food was scarce. The police advised us to assign one person to shop for each coach, but many did not heed to the advice and soon two thirds were gathered around the vendors. There was not much in the baskets. There were the unavoidable boiled eggs, onions, garlic, black radish, olives, and *tahin halva* [sesame sweet] which was quite popular and had many buyers.

What were these vendors told about us we did not know. They would not give us the food until we first paid for them. Surely all of them were Turks. Then we saw Armenians, who had the common sense to bring cigarettes, tobacco and tobacco paper. Their inventory was sold out in a flash. They did not hide their ethnicity, but we were obliged to speak Turkish. They did not speak Armenian. The last ones who arrived were young Armenian vendors who sold dried fruits. Despite the army of policemen, Dr. Miskdjian, who was Catholic and really had relations in Angora, found a way to slip a note to them through one of the boys. Perhaps others who had relations or acquaintances in the city also did the same things.

It seemed that the news of our arrival had already spread in Angora. Small groups of curious people appeared from here and there, but they kept their distance at a certain point. There were Armenians among them as well, and a few were able to approach them, with the excuse to change money. There was not enough change on the vendors and many of us were having difficulty paying for the food that we bought. We were obliged to buy more than we needed to avoid losing 5 or 10 ghurush in change.

It did not take a genius to realize the different attitude of the curious onlookers of Turkish or Armenian origin. The former certainly had a horrible impression of our crowd. The strict surveillance which we were subjected to further confirmed in their eyes the terrible stories that they had heard about us. In general they had a cross look on their face and some looked at us with malice. The Armenians, on the other hand, who no doubt were informed about our identities by the railroad workers of Armenian origin, were surprised by the sheer number of police, soldiers and gendarmes who were deployed to transport such a harmless crowd as ours.

These kind people felt sorry for us and they wished us a comfortable but mostly safe journey. An imminent horror was going to harvest them even before us…

The police obliged us to return to our carriages. I took out my coat, folded it, and sat on it to make myself more comfortable.

It was around noon when the convoy was ready to take off. The *yaylis*, five of them, more agile and light-weight, were soon directed to the uneven and stony path surrounding the meadows. Our carriages started to follow them slowly. The coachmen were making infernal noises to keep the horses on the path. They pleaded, threatened, at time coerced with tender words. Curse words were heard everywhere. There were forty two carriages including *yaylis*. One of the latter, which carried Ibrahim Effendi, an officer, and a policeman was the last caravan. Ibrahim Effendi had ordered the cover down to survey the action more freely.

All the policemen we left in Angora. Only two dozen mounted gendarmes accompanied the caravan on the left and the right side at a certain distance from each other, which of course formed a long line. The two soldiers who accompanied us were good humored and made fun of the coachman for his ignorance.

The suburb we were passing through was left behind. The gendarmes did their best to keep the curious at bay. Soon we plunged into the winding roads surrounded by hills which covered the left side of the city like a cob web. The carts could not maintain their line, became separated from one another, and were scattered here and there. It took a long time to until we arrived at the main Chankiri road. If the caravan passed straight through the city, the road would have been much shorter and it would have saved plenty of misery to the people and the animals. But they did not want to parade us in front the population of the city. And probably it was a good decision. Surely they did the right thing.

Ibrahim Effendi was able to put the caravan in order very quickly, which from now on was to speed forward light-heeled. At the start the road was in a good condition and for a moment we had the illusion that our journey was not going to be as torturous as we imagined. Although our carts were not made to go fast, we jumped each and every time they hit a small stone or pile of dirt, but as long as the road was smooth and even we were not bothered that much.

We glided through vast cultivated fields and borderless meadows. Green was king and under the pleasant sunshine was reigning everywhere. The weather started to become cooler and the shiver made me put on my coat which was serving as a cushion.

Here and there one still could see plows, but sparsely. More often we met herds of sheep, or specially herds if goat. We mostly saw women and children in the fields, and rarely elderly man. Some of the women and the children did the tasks of the animals, in order to compensate for the animals that were confiscated by the government.

The soldier in our cart was certainly a peasant. He could not take off his eyes from the women and children who served as animals. It was obvious that his mind wondered to his own village where it was probably in the same situation. The men were all drafted into the army.

"Are we short of land? For god's sake we fight for more land," he murmured under his nose.

It was not clear if he was doing a monologue or his words were directed at us. In any case, airing on the side of caution, we avoided responding to him.

Later, we heard the same expressions from the Turks of Chankiri. The war was not popular with the Turks of the older generation.

But soon the soldier started to sing. We could not hear the words, as he sang in a very low voice, but the tune was very pleasant and it touched us.

Some of our people were also singing in the other carts. There was no end to the jokes. The jokes went from one cart to the other when the caravan stopped near a water spring to water the horses. Some of us came out of the carts also to quench our thirst.

For almost two hours the road remained smooth like that. Those two hours were relatively comfortable.

But soon the dance started when the road suddenly transformed after an elevation. Many of us had to disembark so the carts could climb the hill. It was a pleasure to walk, in comparison to the torture of riding in the carts. The road had not been repaired for many years and it was full of holes. In front of us lay a cursed journey where the carts were going to go mad out of control. It made us jump out of our wooden seats and then fall down hard on them. In half an hour we all felt beaten to a pulp. The pain in our bones, which was going to accompany us until Chankiri, and was going to last for many days after we arrived, was killing us already.

The soldier in our carriage was indifferent to all of this. This mode of transportation might have been luxurious for him. He was surprised why we were complaining so much. While we changed our positions constantly, hoping to alleviate our discomfort, which we did not succeed, he was seated with folded legs, his gun on his knees, and the bayonet of his gun directed toward father Vartan. The latter was bewildered, trying to protect himself from leaping off wooden seats, which were hammering his bones, as well as from the hopping bayonet which was threatening to pierce his side.

Chapter 19

Descent to Hell

We were saved of unpleasant events while our caravan was dashing forward with the same mad course. The roads and the fields were almost deserted. Once in a while we could see lone peasants, generally on foot, sometimes on donkeys, accompanied by barefoot urchins. We encountered a few groups of men, surely of conscription age, with a small satchel or a parcel of their belongings on their back, heading to Angora to enlist. These men stopped for a second to watch our caravan, and most probably thought we were prisoners of war. Certainly they had the opportunity to see others pass by before us. A freight cart which was coming from the opposite direction and heading to Angora, under the insistence of the gendarmes, was obliged to move aside, until our caravan passed through.

Although at times the road was in a better condition, soon the jolts restarted and our torture continued. We felt lucky when a freight cart stopped. It happened that a strap came loose, or it lost a wheel, or one of the horses tumbled into a ditch. Soon the caravan stopped and all the coachmen helped each other to take care of the problem. It was an especially arduous task to raise a fallen horse to its feet. All the straps and knots had to be loosened, the animal had to be cajoled to stand on its feet, and then it had to be examined for possible injuries. Any scrapes or wounds had to be dressed and then the animal had to be yoked. These steps took time and made plenty of noise.

We took full advantage of those occasions and visited with friends and acquaintances in other carriages. All of them, like us, complained of pain and felt beaten to pulp. Some were like pieces of rag unable to move, slumped in a corner, discouraged, asking when this cursed road would end. We found others walking around the carriages, content to be able to stretch their legs. Our legs were weak and our steps were feeble. Krikor Yesayan tried on one of those occasions to hasten his gait, to pick up a flower, and tumbled down. When we helped him up, he said that he did not feel his legs. We also experienced similar numbness in our legs.

We did not have the chance to approach the *yayli*s to see how the privileged fared. They were far from us at the helm of the caravan, and they were significantly ahead of the rest because of their speed. In comparison, without any shred of doubt, they were traveling in comfort and were not very distressed due to the suspension on their carriages, which significantly diminished the jolts.

Three and a half hours had passed since our departure from Angora and our journey continued with those providential intermissions. The last time we boarded the freight carts, the soldier who was snoozing woke up, looked around, and prepared to go to sleep, when we asked him where were we heading to.

"We are heading to Ravli, but we still have two hours to go."

We found out from him that the carriages from Angora, in general, made two overnight stops, first at Ravli, and then at Kalejik. They left Kalejik early in the morning and made a midway stop at Tuney Khan, and arrived at Chankiri late at night. Of course Behaeddin Bey knew this routine and informed us at the train station of Angora that we had a three day journey ahead of us to our detention camp.

His revered father Vartan, who sat still and motionless all the way, had the advantage over us as he leaned on bales of straw, and still declared.

"I will die if the journey goes on for one more hour."

Probably he had not heard what the soldier had said. We had two more hours until Ravli.

The soldier, before falling asleep, expressed some doubts about how long we might spend in Ravli as there was the possibility that we might continue on to Kalejik during the night.

"How many hours from Ravli?" we inquired.

"The way we are going, it is seven or eight hours," he said with indifference and closed his eyes.

We felt simply crestfallen.

It was four in the afternoon, when finally we arrived to Ravli, our first place of rest, where Komitas Vartabed's "drama" was to begin.

The word, often used and reused, is not correct. It is a huge hyperbole when it refers to the distress which started on the way to our detention camp. Although a group of parakeet repeat again and again that Komitas went mad on route to exile, the truth is that he *did not go mad on the way to exile*. The reason for the collapse of his reason, which later became apparent in Constantinople, is a complex circuitous knot. To solve this knot one has to take into consideration many issues, only one of which could be the detention camp. But this does not mean if it was not for the exile that he was not going to lose his reason. I will have time to reflect on this later. The only thing I would like to mention here is that detention for Komitas and seven others who shared the same luck was that their exile was very short, only 15 days, counting the days of arrest and journey. He was arrested on the same day, the night of Saturday 24 April 1915, and we left Constantinople the following Sunday night. The order for his release came 14 days afterwards, on the morning of Sunday May 9th. He was free to roam one day in Chankiri, without any restrictions, and on Tuesday, May 11th, he left with his seven companions of fortune, to arrive in Constantinople on Saturday night, May 15th.

Komitas' "drama" in exile was an instance of nervousness, or let me call it an intense episode of nervousness, which neither achieved troubling proportions, nor lasted a long time.

His distress, assuming it had not started already, appeared for the first time on the night of April 27th, soon after we arrived at Ravli khan. It was triggered by an act of rudeness on the part of a gendarme and lasted until the night of April 29th, when we already were at Chankiri garrison. The whole thing lasted two nights and two days, with intermissions of different duration, during which he hardly uttered a word.

He was not alone in this state of distress. I already told you about the Hunchag veteran Sako's state of mind. He remained in Sindjan Keoy and was taken to Ayash, and we did not hear from him any more. Much later I heard that he had regained his calm. Among the people who were with us in Chankiri, there were three people who also experienced episodes of nervous distress.

Among them was an elderly friend, Kasbar Cheraz. He was one of the kindest, sweetest and devoted men that I have ever encountered in my life. His distress appeared the night of April 28th, when the freight carts that were transporting us stopped in front of Chankiri garrison.

Exactly at the same time another person lost his reason. He was the one who was arrested by mistake. His name was Vertanes Papazian, the same as the writer Vertanes Papazian. He was a sweet old man. He spent the night on the first floor of the garrison with the distinguished people among us. In the morning, when we saw him, he had regained his composure. We kept him on the ground floor with us. Soon he calmed down and had a quite night.

For both of these men, the distress proved to be transient and was never repeated.

The last person who experienced a nervous reaction was Dr. Krikor Djelal. It happened suddenly, without any obvious external reason, at a café near a rivulet, where we gathered every day, out of the city. It was a place seldom frequented by Turks. The nervous state of Dr. Djelal proved to be the most dangerous, and the one that lasted the longest. His nervousness was accompanied with

Historian Vertanes Papazian

bouts of delusional excitement, which was very difficult to control. By nature a kind, quiet and gentle person, when delusional, he screamed, yelled and threatened everybody and everything around him. Two of Yerevoum's muscular friends, from the *ayingadjis* [tobacco smugglers], were asked to follow Dr. Djelal and serve as sort of nurses. They held down his arms as needed to prevent him causing any harm. Friends and acquaintances gathered around him, as his political party friends tried to appease him with kind words, cajoling him to calm down, but he did not respond, until the episode of the agitation subsided on its own. Following such episodes, he returned to his normal self. I do not know if he remembered those episodes after they passed. In any case we avoided making any remarks to remind him of them.

Luckily, the mayor of the Chankiri was a young man who was the student of Dr. Djelal's brother, Hovsep Djelal in Constantinople, for whom he had deep feelings of respect. The young man decided to help his teacher's brother out of feelings of gratitude toward his teacher. He presented a petition on his behalf stating that Dr. Djelal was sick and presented danger to public safety. He argued that no mental health facilities existed in Chankiri, and that it was advisable to transfer him to Constantinople where he could receive treatment. The governor Asaf Bey also confirmed Dr. Djelal's "madness". The game plan worked and the doctor was allowed to return to Constantinople. This was despite the fact that he was the president of the Hunchag party's executive committee, Constantinople branch.

At the time the Hunchagian party was divided into two opposing factions. Constantinople branch maintained a legitimate policy, while the group abroad and a few in Constantinople adopted more militant stand that was decided at their Costanza conference.

Sabah-Gulian struck a financial agreement with a Kurd, Sherif Pasha in Paris, to engage a few terrorists with orders to kill the members of the cabinet, Talaat, Enver and Djemal in Constantinople. Many were aware of their presence and they were constantly at the café of Cholakh Onnig, in Pangalti. In that café, the presence of many secret agents was felt as well. The government was aware of the plot due to the treason by Arshavir Sahagian. Many of them remained under surveillance for a while and were later arrested. Their friends with whom they kept relations while under surveillance were also arrested. They were 20 people in all who were tried in Constantinople and were hanged a few weeks after our arrest on 2 June 1915. Among this group of 20, there were very few followers of Sabah-Gulian. Others were fulfilling a social duty by being friendly with the terrorists. But the plan was not really a serious one. One of the men who was hanged, Yeremia Manoogian, was closely related to my wife. He was not in agreement with Sabah-Gulian's assassination plan. One day he recounted to me how the terrorists ran out of money and had to pawn their revolvers. Believe me I do not exaggerate any of this.

Due to this schism in the party, the Hunchagian party of Constantinople, for an instance, seemed to have gained the trust of the government. But finally the murderers of the day indiscriminately arrested the ones in Constantinople and abroad and exiled them with us. Mourad was hanged under horrible circumstances in Caesarea, while his tortured body was hardly able to keep a trace of breath. Ardzrouni, Haroutiun Kalfayan, Djangulian, Sako, Nersess Zakarian and others, who were martyred under hideous circumstances, were Hunchag party members who had remained loyal to the legitimate policy line.

Let me close this parenthesis and return to my story.

Chapter 20

Fight Over Water

We reached the station of Ravli khan, after descending on a stony, downhill road. The danger of tumbling off precipices in our coaches, which luckily lasted a short duration, caused us the heaviest hardship on the road. It was not surprising that our arrival was followed by our hurried escape from the coaches, without waiting a second. It was a miracle that no accident happened. The young men jumped out before their coaches stopped. Some fell on the road and were void of enough energy to get away before being trampled by the oncoming horses. Inattentiveness or hurry by any of the coachmen could have caused a disaster.

The men who left the coaches directed their gait toward the khan, a spacious, simple two story square building, void of any architectural style. There were no carvings on the front entrance, nor windows on the façade of the building. There was a simple line, as if drawn by a ruler, showing the separation of the first and second floors. It was obvious that the cells on both floors received their light and fresh air from the courtyard. It looked more like a fort than a building which served human habitation. This was common for those buildings which served as dens for thieves and contrabandists. The color of the walls at one point must have been white, which was still visible in this or that corner, among the multicolor mildew, caused by humidity, which had turned it into a repulsive black.

The surroundings were pleasant, with woody meadows, which shined under the glare of the sun. There was a breeze that shook the trees gently, but soon the wind picked up speed, shaking the trees as if they were intoxicated. There was every indication that we were going to have a cold night. At that time of day the weather was warm and pleasant, the wind was not disturbing, and many of us reclined on the grass or leaned on a tree trunk and breathed in the fresh air with the full capacity of our lungs. A few of us were massaging this or that part of their aching muscles, accompanied by screams of satisfaction and exclamations of pain, intermingled with curse words, the majority of which were directed, rightfully so, at the men who ran the government. One only had to hear Krikor Yesayan!

In general we had the feeling that our bones had left their sockets and it would take time for them to return home. The ones who traveled in *yaylies* were also in pain. Perhaps not as much as we were in, but they also had their fair share of discomfort. They jumped up and down and tumbled all over each other. We saw them around the khan. They had arrived ahead of us. Some of them were leaning on the walls, others were hobbling along the khan. In general they were older people, less interested in the healing magic of nature, which had become a soothing pleasure for us.

The soldiers had also descended and were slowly gathering in small groups, moving toward the sub-commissioners, who remained mounted on their horses on the left side of the road. We could not see Ibrahim Effendi, who was hiding behind overgrown bushes. We could see one or two of his officials. Soon the sub-commissioners also disembarked their horses, threw the bridles at the first soldiers nearby, and disappeared behind the bushes. Judging from the soldiers who opened their meager satchels and started to chew on whatever they had, we assumed that Ibrahim Effendi was also eating.

Like others, I also lay down under a tree, while Khodjasarian rushed to the khan to look for something to eat. Both of us were hungry. We had lost the food we had bought in Angora. The package of food had tumbled under the seat of either Father Vartan or Khodjasarian and remained there more than an hour. The boiled egg got all smashed and turned into an unpleasant and unrecognizable purée. We gave it to the soldiers and the coachmen who were contended with the bread alone.

Lying under that tree, I was following the road which branched into two. The right branch, like a crescent, encircled the khan from the back and joined a double tree lined alley way which extended to a forest covering the horizon. A thick smoke and a few gardens scattered here and there indicated the presence of a village. It was probably the village of Ravli which remained hidden from view.

The left branch, after an interruption in front of the khan, widened and took shape again. It ended in a square, where the coaches that had transported us were parked. The road extended further from the square to our next station, Kalejik, lined by a row of trees. I could not see it any further. The parked coaches covered my vision and I could only see the tips of green and barren mountains.

I was joined on the grass by the arms dealer, Mgrdich Barsamian, a very pleasant fellow and, in such trying circumstances, a courageous companion. Judge for yourself. He was looking for "blessed water". He was referring to *arak* (ouzo). He was annoyed that he could not find any. He was angry at God who created such beautiful nature but did not inhabit it with people who would enjoy his other creation, the arak, and not forbid it under the pretense of offending him.

This large spirited man was looking for his arak, while others were brooding about death…

Ardashes Haroutiunian

Later they took him to Nikomedia (Izmit) from Chankiri, by the orders of the military tribunal. Some Armenians, under torture, had named him as the vendor of the guns found during the search of their homes.

His circumstances were serious and in those days terror was reigning in Nikomedia. Those were the days of tortures for unfortunate Ardashes Haroutiunian and the martyrdom of many like him. It was not even possible to nurture any shred of hope for Mgrdich's freedom. But he did survive.

Months later, in Tarsus, where I insisted on remaining after the departure of Yervant Odian and Karekin Vartabed Khachadourian, I used to speak Greek and they thought I was Greek, until they arrested me at night. A Turkish major had been murdered earlier and they were looking for the murderer everywhere. They found me on the street and threw me in jail… as a murderer. Fortunately the murderer, a young Turkish man, a candidate to become an officer, had murdered the major to defend his honor and gave himself up the next morning. The charge was lifted but they detained me as a runaway from exile. That night I had a big surprise when I met Mgrdich in Tarsus jail. They had brought him there two days earlier, in the company of vagabonds.

They gave this humiliating name (vagabond) to those exiles who had no families with them.

He screeched with happiness.

"I am glad you came. Look at those mourners," he pointed to the people surrounding him.

Truly all of them had teary eyes and looked sad. Mgrdich was scared that he might become melancholic as well.

He was especially annoyed by two people who pretended to be from Selanik. Actually they were from Van, and they were trying to hide their identity. The events of Van were widely publicized and to avoid additional hardship, the exiled of Van were obliged to cover their places of origin. On every occasion and everywhere they pretended to be from "Selanik". Their special "sweet" dialect betrayed them but the Turks were not aware of such nuances. They defended themselves by saying not to worry, they did not mind being vagabonds. Vagabonds were the kings of the roads these days.

Truly our lonely situation, which was not void of many disadvantages, at least gave us a half-freedom in comparison to those who had wives, children and elders, especially young girls with them.

We spent a joyful night, becoming a nuisance to others.

Two days later we were put on the road together once more. We stayed together until the desert of Meskene, where luck was going to separate us once more. He survived as well.

Khodjasarian returned with fresh bread and a big piece of *khavurma,* also *tahin halva,* which after that day was going to be our daily diet. Whatever he bought for two was enough for three. He could not buy crushed salt. Instead, he bought a piece of mineral salt that we had to lick after each bite of *khavurma.* Soon we were thirsty and *tahin halva* made it worse. All three of us got up and went to the square where we had noticed a well.

The majority of our people were in the khan at that time. There were hardly two dozen people outside. Some were lying under the trees, while others were walking around. The wind at times picked speed, but the weather remained pleasant and we did not shiver.

The square always remained hidden from our sight because of the coaches. We could not see the horses, but all of them were detached from their coaches. A huge noise was coming from that direction. Some of our people who were thirsty like us had gone to fetch water but were returning empty handed.

"If you are going to get water, do not go. It is impossible to get any."

We heard from them that a big argument had broken out between the gendarmes and the coachmen. Each of them tried to give water to their horses first. There was limited access to the water. The coachmen wanted to have priority to water their 84 horses. The gendarmes wanted to have priority for their animals.

This was the reason for the heated argument which seemed to be picking steam.

Confused, we stood around for a while. Suddenly, we were approached by Armen Dorian and Mihran Basturmadjian who, taking advantage of the ongoing argument, had fetched a bucket full of water and were about to get away as they approached us.

At the same time Komitas Vartabed, Father Housig, architect Simon Melkonian, Yervant Chavoushian and the imperial mint official Garabed Deuvletian, who was also a first-class drama actor in Constantinople, were also there. There were others surrounding them as well, but I cannot recall their names for sure. They were all thirsty and coming to have water.

Chavoushian said that there was a huge barrel of water inside the khan, but some said it smelled bad. The cups provided by the khan owner also looked dirty so they declined to drink from them and came outside to drink from the well.

Among all the most impatient people was Komitas. When he saw the clear water, he exclaimed with happiness. Bending his head forward, he started to jump up and down, rubbing his hands as he always did in moments of excitement. His gaze was fixed on the sparkling water, as if there was no world beyond that bucket full of water.

To drink from that bucket turned out to be a problem. We did not have any cups to take some water. We did not want to use our hands. They were not washed for a long time, and being rubbed here and there, they had turned black, leaving the impression that we had gloves on. The most convenient way was to lift the bucket to the mouth of the vartabed so that he could drink.

Exactly at the moment the vartabed approached the bucket and held it with his two hands while others lifted it for him, a mounted gendarme approached without being noticed by us. With a rude attack he snatched the bucket from the hands of Basturmadjian and Dorian. It was fortunate that the metal rim on that heavy bucket did not hit Komitas' nor anybody else's head. The consequences could have been very serious. But Komitas was seriously frightened. He retreated back a few steps and wrapped his right arm around his head to protect it from further attacks. His face was splashed with water and it was dripping down his beard. Yervant Chavoushian, who was standing just beside him, was even wetter.

This incident happened with such speed that many of us did not realize what exactly went on. The bucket was on the floor, empty, and all our gazes were on it.

Komitas was simply bewildered. He stood there motionless, as if he had turned into stone. He did not notice the handkerchief that our friends were offering him to wipe his face dry. In his eyes there was an expression, not of fear, but one of astonished surprise, and he was unable to take his eyes off the gendarme. The latter, bellowing under his nose, bent down, took the bucket, and was about to leave, when Ibrahim Effendi, who noticed the incident with his all seeing eyes, hurriedly approached us and stopped the gendarme.

"Where are you taking that bucket?" he asked.

"I am going to give water to our *hayvans* [animals]".

"*Evela bu hayvanlare* [first to these animals]" yelled Ibrahim Effendi, ordering him to put down the bucket.

He said this in an ordinary tone. I do not think that it occurred to him that his words could have been offensive to us. He could have easily said "*Evel bunlare* [first to them]." I do not think he used this word to insult us intentionally. Turkish officials often used it due to a lack of education, lack of courtesy, or sheer habit. Our superiors used it with their subordinates or workers to express discontent when they noticed a shortcoming.

The gendarme left with the usual incomprehensible groan in his mouth. The curses remained in between his teeth when he left. Komitas' eyes remained fixated on him until he disappeared.

Ibrahim Effendi walked to the square, the empty bucket in his hand. He stopped the arguments between the gendarmes and the coachmen. On his orders, the coachmen brought us four buckets out of six available, asking us to quench our thirst quickly.

We naturally hurried. With the appearance of a primordial ladle, which was found near the grocer in the khan, it became much easier to drink the water from the bucket. We washed the ladle not with soap, the latter was a dream commodity in Ravli station, but with the dirt of the earth.

Komitas, who just a short while earlier was the thirstiest and least patient man amongst us, was offered the first ladle of water. He refused it and silently entered the khan.

Chapter 21

Komitas Unstuck

Soon we put the incident with the gendarme and Komitas' reaction to it behind us. The witnesses of the event did not pay much attention to the fact that Komitas refused water and then quietly entered the khan. Under the circumstances, on our way to a detention camp, the cruel and rude action by a gendarme was not seen as an extraordinary occurrence in the eyes of the detainees. It was part of the course, especially in Turkey. Even in civilized countries this would not have been a surprise. Everywhere, and in every nation of the world, gendarmes are brutal, to put it mildly.

We were preoccupied with something else. Turkish villagers had come with carefully tied bundles of straw. By tying a few bales with each other, they explained to us, we could create cushions at the bottom of the coaches. They swore *"vallahi, billahi"* [honest to God] that it would absorb the jolts of the road and our ride would be much more comfortable.

Mgrdich had already gone to deal with the villagers, while Khodjasarian and I were about to follow him, when Kelegian approached us and inquired about Komitas. He informed us that the vartabed looked "bizarre," refused to eat, cast a suspicious look on anything that moved, especially people who came in and out of the khan.

We recounted the event in a few words, without making a secret that the main culprits of the incident were Dorian and Basturmadjian. We also told him about the intervention by Ibrahim Effendi, the reprimand that he had hurled at the gendarme, and the tasteless words with which he honored us.

Kelegian took a sigh of relief. He and others inside the khan had thought that an insult was directed at Komitas personally. The gendarme had not directed any insult to either Komitas or to any one else in particular. Of course he had noticed Dorian and Basdurmadjian when they had snatched the bucket. They were standing near Komitas, and the gendarme had not said anything even to them. He was simply trying to retrieve the bucket.

"We were concerned that it might have been a more serious affair," replied Kelegian.

He looked reassured and content.

While this conversation was going on, the villagers had sold all the straw and there was nothing else to do but to follow Kelegian inside the khan. The wind was now blowing with gusto and we could feel the cold. The people reclining here and there on the straws bales were on their feet. A few were coming back from the coaches. They had gone to spread the straw on the wooden floors. Some had finished doing this and were returning back to the khan.

Mikayel Shamdandjian was one of them. He, with his two friends from Uskudar on this journey, was proudly telling Kelegian that they had organized their coach in such a way that they were sure to be protected from the jolts and jerks of the road. They had even bought more straw than they needed for that purpose.

But Kelegian, who was one of the lucky ones to travel with *yaylies*, had another concern. At one point he had brought the inappropriate attitude of some of the people in our caravan to our attention. We looked more like people going on a picnic than exile. He especially mentioned those who were singing, like Armen Dorian, who really sang frequently, most of the time with a pleasant voice in French.

He was not alone in this opinion. Many others shared his views. They were worried and disturbed. Some were even scared that the joyful uncaring demeanor adopted by some of us, which at times became unpleasantly noisy, could irritate the officials who were accompanying us and change their tactful behavior towards us. Shamdandjian and Khodjasarian also shared this view. But Kelegian's thoughts went further. He was not concerned by a change of attitude by the officials.

"They are carriers of orders. They will not say anything but they will not forget anything either. They will report to Constantinople... we should worry about them... the ones who decided on our exile did not send us for a joyous ride. Our lighthearted attitude could call them to task and result in more severe orders in coming days."

This idea was not shared by everyone amongst us. This issue was going to become a bone of contention in Chankiri, where some of us would continue to be extremely careful and circumspect, while others would give into an unbridled lifestyle. This situation continued as long as we remained unaware and unwary of our fate and the fate of the Armenian people living in Turkey as a whole. But as the news worsened and the killings and mass deportations started, when groups were separated from us and were martyred, the mood soon changed and everyone became a "lamb". By then the "prodigious" ones were taken away, and the sad luck that befell them was not a secret for the remaining ones.

Of course there always remained differences of opinion, and it was a sheer matter of optimism and pessimism.

When we entered the khan, we saw Komitas seated on one of those Turkish café chairs, low and without back rest, near a cell at the left side of the hall. He was in an obviously distressed state. Seated on stools surrounding Komitas were Dr. Torkomian, Dr. Djevahirian, Rev. Keropian, Balakian Vartabed and others. Nobody spoke. Komitas hardly looked at us when we passed by him. Kelegian remained with them, while I left with Khodjasarian and joined a group of acquaintances.

By then the majority were in the khan. Whoever were outside gradually came in because of the cold. Some were able to find a stool and sit down. Others reclined on mats in front of the cells and conversed in groups. Komitas' unusual state did not draw much attention and the incident outside was not discussed widely.

The majority had eaten. Some people who had come in late could not find any food to buy. The grocer sent a person to bring whatever food was available in the village. The people who remained hungry were waiting for the return of the man bringing more food.

The main subject of conversation was the village, or more correctly, the two villages attached to each other and separated by vast gardens. They were not noticeable from the khan. The grocer had told our friends their names were *Dumanli* [smoky] and *Dumansuz* [without smoke]. We did not know if they were official names or just nicknames to tell the two villages apart. But it was very important to tell them apart.

Only women lived in Dumanli, and only their men (husbands, fathers, brothers, male relations and mature boys) lived in Dumansuz.

None of the men could enter Dumanli even to see their wives, their parents, or their daughters, though the women were free to go into Dumansuz anytime they wanted. They brought food or sent it with the children to the men. The fire was always on in the houses of Dumanli, and the smoke was visible. This is where they got their names. It was natural that strange men were forbidden from entering the village as well. This was not a joke. If anyone dared to enter Dumanli, the women attacked the person in a group with cudgels, and with their heavy wooden shoes, regardless who the man was who broke the law, even if he was one of their husbands or brothers. The grocer continued to explain that the man could even be seriously injured if he was attacked with one of the tools used to turn the soil before planting.

When we first heard this story, one of us said that upon arrival at the station, one of the gendarmes did warn them against walking to the village, informing that no man could enter that village, and if they did, they could encounter problems. They did not believe the gendarme, thinking that the gendarme made up the story so we would not run away from the khan.

Others had seen a man in the khan who had been injured by the women of Dumanli. He was a young Turkish man from Kastemuni. He was refused enlistment in Angora due to a physical problem. On his way back he was probably hungry when he saw the smoke coming out of the village and went there to find food. However, instead of getting food, he was beaten and injured on his head.

Kechian and a few "know it alls" were reclined on a mat and were trying to understand the mystery of this village. There was no consensus and this kind of pedantic discussion turned into a full blown argument. The majority were of the opinion that the population of these villages were the descendants of the Amazons. Kechian also thought along such lines and pointed out that the Amazon people were originally from Cappatocia so that a branch could have come here to settle.

I still remember months later, when I encountered a similar village at the foot of the Amanos mountains, immediately after I had left Islahiye. I was with a group of exiled Armenians and we were hungry. We could not get food in Islahiye. We had descended into a vast field. The first thing that we had noticed was a village whose name we could never know. It was built like an amphitheatre on our left side. With the permission of the gendarme who was guarding us, one of us went to the village with the hope of finding bread. He returned empty handed with his head injured and bleeding. The village was inhabited by women only. Probably the village where the men lived was not very far, but the man had gone to the first village and was beaten by the women.

The men returned from Dumansuz with food. The young fellow who was injured by the women of Dumanli was accompanying him. The grocer who was a good natured elderly man took that man as a helper, to show him as a curiosity object. I grew gray here but never dared to enter Dumanli, while this one was courageous and did it in one day. If you do not believe me you just have to look at his head. Truly half of the fellow's head was wrapped in bandages.

Exactly at that time we heard Komitas' voice and we turned to see him.

"Did the gendarme do that?" he asked pointing at the man with his right index finger.

He repeated this question a few times. I do not recall what they answered him. He looked disturbed. The gaze of his eyes caused distress to onlookers. But the fact that he started to communicate was seen as a reassuring sign. He had not said a word since he entered the khan.

The fear of the gendarme started to germinate in his mind and became the common denominator in his nervous breakdown. The latter took an acute form during the night and the day after.

Soon our attention was distracted from Komitas. We were informed by the people outside that the coaches were being yoked and lined up. At the same time two gendarmes entered the khan and informed us that we would be moving soon and invited us to come out as soon as possible.

When we came out of the khan the soldiers were standing near the coaches. We could not see Ibrahim Effendi, but we could hear his voice. He was giving orders left and right to the gendarmes and to the coachmen. The latter insisted that we hurry, but we were having hard time to find the coach and passengers with whom we had come to Ravli. The ones who traveled on *yaylies* had no difficulty. As the chaos got worse Ibrahim Effendie's orders became louder. One of the gendarmes asked what we were waiting for? We told them that we were looking for our coaches.

"They are all the same. Get in the one beside you."

The first coach that was beside us was lined up by layers and layers of straw. We boarded it, Der Vartan, Khodjasarian and myself, and we were pleased with our unexpected luck. The soldier was not the same, but he was as kind as the first one, and less husky, therefore taking up less space. The men sat down and congratulated us on our choice of coach.

It was Shamdandjian's coach that were lucky to have occupied. Later he refused to believe that our finger was not in this plot. Next morning we let him have it, but the first allure to travel on the straw was gone. During the mad dash, the bales had crumbled and turned into a pile of loose straw. Furthermore, the wind caused a storm of prickles, which blinded the eyes, and made even conversation impossible. Anyone who dared to open their mouth would choke. The number of people who kept coughing was large.

We brought the prickles of straw with us to Chankiri. It took attentive and methodical work to clean them out of our clothes, underwear, even our body and hair. I do not remember the mustaches and the beards, but for many like myself, the first purchase in Chankiri was a comb.

Chapter 22

Broken Bones, Tortured Souls:
Friends in Misery

We left Ravli late in the evening when there was still light. We were all annoyed. We preferred to spend the night in the khan, despite the dirty mats and the lack of pillows and covers. Our broken bodies could have used a night's rest to recover.

There were elderly and sick people among us. We were worried about the Miskdjian brothers, the doctor and the pharmacist, who both suffered chest pain. Varoujan, who was their travel mate, was scared that one or the other was going to have an attack and remain on the road.

The eldest brother, Mihran, of the three Kayekdjian brothers, was also sick. Then there were the older Vertanes Papazian, almost eighty years old, and Krikor agha Ohnigian, who was accompanied by his three sons. Of course there were also others whom we did not notice.

Komitas Vartabed's nervousness was also a source of concern. But we did not see him outside.

As we dreaded, the coaches started their dance macabre as we hit the road. I do not want to say more about the torture of our bones. After sundown, when it was dark, the mad dash of the caravan really turned into a rally.

Luckily, when the surrounding fields were flat, the coachmen left the road and went through the fields. Those were relatively calm moments, but they did not last long, as we soon returned to the road and the jolts started.

When we went through cultivated fields, we heard complaints rising from here and there, often from the women who were working the fields. Some had long strings of curse words. We did not know who they were directed at, us or the coachmen. Despite these screams, Ibrahim Effendi went back and forth in his *yayli,* surveying the caravan without caring about the tilled fields. Often his voice was heard ordering the coachmen to lash the horses. People did everything to encourage the animals to hurry.

Others were also disgusted with Ibrahim Effendi.

"He will not shut up until he slaughters the animals" complained our coachman, referring to Ibrahim Effendi. The man was worried about his horses. He was not worried about the coach. The latter could be repaired. However, because of the war, the military authorities had confiscated anything that moved on four legs. To find a horse that was alive and could move its tail was not an easy matter.

This leg of the trip proved to be worse than the Angora-Ravli portion of the road. The jolts of the coaches were the same, but it was daytime and we were not cold. On the way to Kalejik, the cold of spring nights set in as soon as it was dark. Some of us had only light clothes and no coats. None of us had warm underwear, and our coats were unable to keep us warm against the shiver.

Soon fear was going to add to the cold.

The caravan was able to keep its fast pace for a long while, alternatively running through the roads and fields. The moon was shining and the coachmen were able to move without difficulties, regardless of ongoing orders from Ibrahim Effendi to go faster. The road became a nightmare when we approached the mountains that covered the horizon, and the winding road that went through them. The moon-light did not penetrate the road winding through high boulders, and we could not see the sky because of them.

The top of the trees looked like ghosts, and our imaginations turned them into giants of fairy tales or legendary monsters.

It was not a road but an underground tunnel, dark like black asphalt. Among the boulders, above our heads, the overgrown wild bushes on the crevices of the rocks took funny shapes, which made us very suspicious and scared.

Later, we were not surprised when Balakian Vartabed described the horror that Komitas experienced on the road. Komitas saw gendarmes hidden behind every tree, and every boulder. Panic stricken, he held his head with his two hands, hiding it under the cover of his coat and asking Balakian Vartabed to recite prayers for him. Balakian also experienced similar illusions, seeing thieves with guns in their hands hidden behind the trees, ready to fire.

Others had more tragic worries as they told us later. That winding road could have been an ideal place to slaughter us, if that was the intention of our captors.

Thank goodness it did not last very long. Soon we left it all behind us and entered a field where the road was in a better shape. Ibrahim Effendi gave permission for a short break so that the coachmen could fill the horses' bridles with straw and barley, which they stole from a village, simply by robbing a barley granary and helping themselves to bundles of straw. The watchmen's alarm woke up the women of the village and an argument broke out. The winners were the coachmen. The gendarmes came to their rescue and convinced the villagers that their action was a necessity for the country and the government. What an orderly country Turkey is...

We were not allowed to leave the coaches because it was night time. But orderliness is not an Armenian virtue. Many found a way to leave the coaches. They used the excuse of going to the bathroom. Soon the cold forced them to return.

The race continued, always on the road, until one of the coaches lost a wheel and we had a second break. The coachmen tried to help each other to repair the problem, but soon Ibrahim Effendi ordered the coach out of the way, which took half an hour. The passengers of that coach rode in the others and the caravan continued its journey.

One hour after midnight we heard from another coach that we would soon be arriving at Kalejik.

Chapter 23

Gendarmes at Work

We could not see the town of Kalejik at that late hour of night. The khan where we were going to spend the night was located on a height. It was a two story ugly building. They were not expecting us. The workers at the khan were not forewarned about our arrival, or this is what we thought. That suited us fine. That meant we would be saved from unnecessary formalities.

Soon two policemen appeared and they went to meet Ibrahim Effendi who arrived later. His *yayli* was parked at the entrance of the khan. We did not know why they were there. Soon we could hear the outraged angry voice and curses of Ibrahim Effendi, which made them regret being there. The two of them remained silent. When they tried to argue their point, this outraged Ibrahim Effendi even more.

The coaches were covering our line of vision and we could not hear what was being said. The coachmen told us why they were arguing. Ibrahim Effendi had sent a telegram ordering them to keep the khan free, but they did not heed to the order. Truly the khan was full as we arrived. There was a market fair the next day and the villagers had gathered there the night before. Some of them had already gone to sleep, others had just arrived and were resting here and there. Some were drinking coffee, others were preparing to sleep.

The policemen who had come from the village were returning when Ibrahim Effendi called them back. A few of the sub-commissioners also joined them. Ibrahim Effendi took a few of the armed soldiers with him and went into the khan.

We could not see what was going on. From the curse words, loud screams and the yelling, we could imagine the scene inside. They had ordered the people to leave the khan and were using their whips and force to carry out their orders. Some even did not have time to take their *yemenis* [shoes] and came out barefoot. Others left their coat or head cover inside. They would not leave until they recovered their belongings, while the whip was at work and new groups were being forced out.

These Turkish villagers were being exposed to the same treatment that was going to befall expatriated Armenians. At least they were forewarned of our arrival. The ones who had nothing inside hurried to leave the scene. However, they were surprised and turned their heads to observe the unusual traffic of so many coaches, as well as our crowd, and the rows of soldiers guarding the elevation.

The villagers saw that we were not prisoners of war. They also noticed the presence of clergy among us. They figured that we were Armenians, and each one of them came to an individual conclusion as to who we were. Of course they were annoyed that their rest was disrupted for a group of *giavurs* [infidels], but they were careful not to voice any complaints. Apart from those who claimed they left their belongings inside the khan and were insisting on getting them back, the rest soon disappeared.

Only at that time did we appreciate the kind of accommodating attitude that we were privileged to receive since we left Constantinople. The groups of other exiles who were going to follow us at short intervals were given different treatment: they were going to be exposed to the rule of the whip on unending roads of torture and death.

Finally the khan was empty. The gendarmes threw out the remaining shoes, head covers, and bundles. The peasants waiting for their belongings tried to find their property among that mixed up mass. It was not an easy task. Some of them cursed and mumbled. With the sudden appearance of Ibrahim Effendi, who was bursting with anger and in a threatening mood, the villagers thought it wiser to collect everything and sort things out somewhere else.

Many people like me hurried to enter the khan. We were exhausted, cold and sleepy. As soon as we entered the door, our first impulse was to step back, and if the crowd following us did not push behind us, perhaps we would have left without giving it a second thought.

The thick smoke of the cigars, cigarettes, and hubble-bubbles filled the lower hall and served as a screen to cover the only oil lamp hanging from the ceiling, with its dim light lighting the room. It was as if we were in a mineral water bath. We groped along, vaguely making each other out. In the dark we felt we were stepping on soft things, squashing them with our shoes, without knowing what they were.

They were left over fruits, different foodstuffs, bread and trash, which the villagers left in their hurry to vacate the place. There was a heavy and unpleasant scent in the air.

But in comparison to the biting cold outside, it was warm and whoever did not have a breathing problem soon got used to it.

The khan consisted of that ground floor where we entered and also served as a coffee house, plus an upper floor. The ground floor was a big square room. At the front, left and right sides, there were risings, covered with torn dirty pieces of rugs and grass mats, which gave the impression of cushions. Two columns, or more correctly, two tree trunks evened out with hatchets, served as columns to support the top floor, which served as sleeping cells. Shamdandjian and others went up to check. Others who preceded them came down and described the situation as unbearable. On the top floor, where the cells were, the smoke had turned into a thick cloud and it had become impossible to breathe. There was hardly room for twenty people in those cells.

Krikor Yesayan, Ardzrouni and others preferred to remain on the lower floor, near one of the columns, on a mat. Yesayan found another mat which we spread near this one and we could not wait to recline. We used our coats as half-mattresses and half-covers, our shoes as pillows, and we lay down and were asleep in no time.

It was loud and not all had come in. All the available places were occupied and the late-comers encountered difficulty to find a place. I remember Kechian soon laid open his bedding and lay down near the second column without undressing. Later he bragged that his bed served five-six people whenever he had an opportunity to use it. This was a hyperbole. Six years later, in 1921, he exaggerated the story further, stating that he shared his bed with "ten fat fellows" in Kalejik. He and his brother-in-law, Dr. Djevahirian, were always together on that bed. Although it was a big bed, both of them were unusually fat people and as much as they tried to sleep side-by-side, their layers of fat drooped over, out of the bed.

Soon they brought in Dr. Miskdjian, who was unable to walk, and took him upstairs. His brother, who was almost in a similar state, joined him as well. Varoujan, who did not leave them, came down to look for Dr. Torkomian, and they rushed up to the patients.

There was another Catholic young man, his name was Karakash, who by trade was a shirt presser. He was arrested in Pera and was mixed in our crowd. He was not a person who would mingle in national affairs. He was probably the victim of a personal vendetta. He had problems with his stomach and the jolts of the road had further upset his fragile state. He was vomiting non-stop. A space was cleared for him in one of the corners on the main floor. It was impossible to bring him upstairs.

The last person that I remember entering the khan was Komitas. He came in with Balakian. He simply roared when he saw the thick smoke in the room. Many of us continued to smoke. In daily life even the sight of an unsmoked cigarette irritated Komitas. They took him upstairs against his will. As he climbed the stairs the smoke was thicker.

Soon my eyes were closed and I fell asleep.

In the morning Ardzrouni tried to wake me up stating that it was late, but he did not succeed. I glanced around, saw others sleeping, and decided to remain put. Of course we could not stay there forever and we finally got up. We were frozen stiff during the night and it took a while to find our feet. Our first steps were real torture. I hoped for sun, but when I went out, I was disappointed. It was as gloomy and cold as the night before.

The carts had disappeared from the square. We were told that they had descended to the valley and we had to follow them there. The road that brought us to Kalejik did a semicircle and went down to an open valley, and from there it went to Chankiri. We had a long and dusty downhill slope in front of us. I could see many people already walking on it. There was no order to move yet, and many of us, the gendarme and coachmen, were still hanging around. The soldiers were around the square, some of them standing, others seated casually. We had the impression that we were in a besieged war zone.

With Krikor Yesayan we washed ourselves near a water well. We had no towels. Yesayan pulled his shirt out of his pants and wiped his face dry with the skirts of his shirt. I had no time to do the same. People were looking at us and laughing hilariously. His face was dirtier than before. His shirt had collected so much dirt and dust that his face was almost black. He had to wash again.

Part of the square had turned into a market place and was full of bustle. The villagers who were evicted from the khan were there and were busy doing business. They were selling everything, different kinds of food, so that we were able to have a nice breakfast. Then we bought molasses. Khodjasarian advised us to do so. He said it would keep our chests warm. That purchase gave rise to an argument. One of the vendors, after taking our money, did not agree to change the bottle which smelled of petroleum. The other peasants were kinder. This one seemed to have been one of those who were whipped the night before and harbored a grudge against us. The issue was resolved after a gendarme interfered and made the vendor change the bottle.

At that time we saw Komitas around us and he was alone which reassured us. He did not have people guarding him, therefore we thought he was doing well. He bowed with reverence to one of the gendarmes who brought back the bottle of molasses from the vendor.

Few of the gendarmes were also shopping in the same place as we were. Komitas greeted all of them with such reverence and humility that some of us, especially those who did not know about his nervous breakdown, suspected that he was making fun of them. But he was serious, if we could call it serious, given the emotional distress with which he was struggling. He was advising us to do the same and was surprised that we did not worry about the gendarmes.

It was obvious that he continued to fear the gendarmes, despite his outwardly calm look. A while later he started to show the same kind of humble reverence to the strangers who passed by. They looked at him surprised, shook their head, and moved away without knowing what was going on. It was obvious that he mistook them for gendarmes. The night before he had done the same thing. He mistook the trees for the gendarmes. That was when we dashed through the tunnel in the dark of night.

News started to arrive from here and there. We learned that two hundred Armenian families lived in Kalejik. In those days they had no clue what fate was awaiting them. Soon the terror was going to harvest their men and turn the women into objects of pleasure for Turkish gendarmes. They were good wine makers. The reputation of their wines had arrived in Chankiri. When we were in Chankiri and had permission to live in the city, some of our friends ordered the coachmen to bring wine from Kalejik. The Armenians had heard from the Turks evicted that night that a big group of Armenians were in the khan and among them were clergymen. Those kind people brought mattresses and covers for the clergy. But the gendarmes did not allow them to go in the khan. However, with the permission of Ibrahim

Effendi, the gendarmes took the mattresses and covers to the top floor. The sick and the clergy were able to spend a comfortable night because of them. Others also took advantage of the beds.

We did not see the Miskdjian brothers that morning. But we heard from Varoujan that they had a good night and the crisis had passed. Dr. Torkomian and other doctors took turns through the night to keep them under observation.

Komitas also had calmed down and was able to sleep.

Karakash had slept poorly, causing discomfort to others, but in the morning they observed that he was calmer. He was among the first who had descended into the valley.

Chapter 24

Corrected Mistake

A group of Armenians had come from Kalejik and were trying to contact us. They were careful not so much for their own safety as our own: they did not wish to cause us any undue problems. They were curious to know why we were being taken to Chankiri in such a large group. We did not show any signs of distress or wary. We freely roamed the square and the market, and happily conversed with each other and joked around. But they had noticed the military surveillance all around the square. The only open road available to us was the dusty, arid, downhill path to the valley.

We also wanted to have some information on Kalejik, which remained hidden from our vision behind a small protuberance of mountains which covered the horizon. The little town remained hidden behind them. We did not have time to approach those Armenians. We heard that a gendarme had arrived on horseback from Angora bearing news related to us.

The source of the news was Haroutiun Kalfayan, a young man from Uskudar. We gathered around him but he knew no more. Upon arrival the gendarme had asked for Ibrahim Effendi and was told that he had descended into the valley. The gendarme followed him without saying anything.

We lost interest in the market place. The news led to much speculation. The optimists among us thought that the gendarme was the harbinger of good news, that he might have brought orders for our release and return to Constantinople.

When we arrived at the khan, there were still a few groups there. Perhaps we were two dozen people, not more. The rest were in the valley and none of them were coming back. The ones who were still near the khan had no idea of the message that the gendarme brought with him.

Komitas was also there. We were surprised to see him. His travel companions and the people by whom he was usually surrounded had all descended to the valley.

Komitas also started to head down the valley when he noticed the arrival of the gendarme at the khan. When he saw the latter heading down the valley, he changed his mind and turned back.

Soon our uncertainties were going to dissipate. We saw Ibrahim Effendi with the gendarme bearing news in the square. Accompanying them was Hunchag party member Ardzrouni. As they were passing in front of us, we asked the latter what was the matter.

"I don't know," he answered. "It seems that they are taking me back."

For a brief while we had the illusion that Ardzrouni was being freed by being called back to Constantinople. This made us happy. At least one of us was being freed. The freedom granted to one would open the doors for others. But soon the clarification followed. Ardzrouni's name was on the list to go to Ayash. Because of a mistake, he was in the group being exiled in Chankiri. He was going to be taken back to Angora and then to Ayash.

We approached Ardzrouni as a group. They did not interfere with our attempts to say goodbye to him. He did not seem to be affected by this decision. Contrary, he was happy that he would be joining his political friends from whom he was separated. He was happy to join his friend Sako with whom he had close ties.

Taking advantage of the situation, we sent our best regards to our friends in Ayash, and we hugged and gave him our best wishes for a safe journey. We were ordered to descend to the valley immediately. While we were descending down the slope, they took him inside the khan, and we did not see his departure.

Ardzrouni left a legacy as graphiti in Osman khan in the town of Ayash. He and Miridjan Artinian, the type-setter of the English daily of Constantinople, *Levant Herald*. nursed Sako, who was sick with pneumonia, and was brought to the khan from the garrison of Sari Kheshla. Dr. Daghavarian, accompanied by a policeman, went daily from the garrison to Osman khan to attend to the patient. In the two diaries he left, he states that "...Half way, from Kalayjik (Kalejik), they took me back to Angora, kept me in jail for four days, and then transferred me here to Ayash near the others, etc..." Sako also left the following note in

Hrant (Melkon Gurdjian)

Osman khan. "I recovered after three weeks of illness and today I return to my garrison jail, Sako."[99]

Both of the notes were dated as 23 May 1915. Sako and Ardzrouni had two months to live when they wrote those notes. During the last days of July they were going to be martyred, side by side, with 28 other friends, in the ill-famed valley of Elma Dagh. The death of the 30 men was the most gruesome of this 1915 drama. Let me tell you in a few words how it happened. After an official salvo, half dead, half alive, some of the living were buried in a huge prepared *hendeg* [pit]. Apart from Ardzrouni and Sako, there were Mihrtad Haygazn, Hovaness Keledjian, Teodor Mendzigian, Khachig Idaredjian, Melkon Gurdjian, (Hrant), Siamanto, Kegham Parseghian, Shavarsh Krisian, Hampartsoum Hampartsoumian, Yenovk Shahen, Krikor Torosian (Gigo), Dikran Cheogiurian, Dr. Garabed Pashayan, Parounag Feroukhan, and the janitor and coffee maker of the newspaper *Azadamard,* Balasan, who was a mere Tashnag sympathizer. Balasan was of Persian origin, Muslim by religion, but spoke Armenian. We were not able to verify the names of the remaining 13 people.

When we were descending into the valley, Komitas stayed with us for a while. He looked extremely upset and emotional, and was shaking his hands and talking to himself. He wanted to know "why the gendarme took Ardzrouni." We explained the reason to him. I do not think he heard what we said. He moved his lips but no words came out of his mouth. We could feel the inner torment that he was going through, but we could not reach him.

Then we passed him and did not see him. Soon we heard his voice, this time clear and loud. "Clear away, open the way," he said.

We thought there was a gendarme coming behind us. We looked back to the khan and could see no one. Something was following us, but it was a withered and sickly donkey with thin and shaky legs going to the valley where the grass was abundant.

Krikor Torosian

Komitas was standing there, with the skirt of his coat folded around his waist. As the animal approached him, he bent down in a gesture of respect and gave a long salute with his hands. He turned to us and told us to wait and let the gendarme pass. He was referring to the donkey.

The scene looked comical and some who did not know his state of mind laughed, thinking that he was joking and being sarcastic. But we knew otherwise and the sadness of the situation gripped our hearts.

This was the last incident with the gendarmes. On the road to Chankiri his fear and wariness was going to take another dimension.

When we came down to the valley the coaches were yoked and lined up on the road ready to take off. Most of our friends were on the meadows. Soon they encircled us to gather news about Ardzrouni. We told them the truth, and we added that Ardzrouni did not seem distressed.

A new worry started to form in our minds. Many figured that there was a difference between the two detention locations. Otherwise, why would they take him to Ayash? Chankiri could also have served as a detention center.

Many among us were of the opinion that the ones who were sent to Ayash were seen as "more dangerous". This was true to a certain degree. The majority of the active revolutionaries, senior or junior members of the party, were among them. Among them were also people who did not have any ties to national or governmental affairs. These people, in comparison to some of us interned in Chankiri, were not "more dangerous". These thoughts confused us and it became difficult to reach any conclusions.

We did not have much time to hammer the problem further. Soon we were informed that we would be leaving. Later, in Chankiri, we were going to debate this issue at length. After our arrival there, two people, Dr. Boghosian and the bookbinder Onnig Maghazajian, were brought to Chankiri, stating that they were sent to Ayash by mistake. It was the last undeniable sign that there was a difference between these two locations of exile.

We started to ride our coaches and saw Ibrahim Effendi for the last time. He was giving instructions to sub-commissioners under whose command our caravan was going to travel the last leg of its journey from Kalejik to Chankiri. Before our caravan would set off, he ordered the coachmen to disperse the curious onlookers who descended to the valley. There were certainly Armenians among them. This was his last show of power. After the disappearance of the curious onlookers, he hurriedly went to the khan and returned to Angora.

The coachmen were happy to give us the news. With his departure they were going to be free from his orders.

We left Kalejik at eight o'clock in the morning on Thursday April 28th. It was a dark and oppressive day. We had a twelve hour road trip ahead of us. We thought of it as twelve hours of torture. But in comparison to the other days, this last leg of the journey was not as bad as we expected.

Worried Sick. Komitas in Agony

Soon we took off from Kalejik without seeing the town. After traveling a distance, we saw it through rugged hills for a few seconds. The ancient fort, after which it was named, looked dilapidated and was mostly blocked from our vision.

The road to Chankiri was in a relatively better shape. For a long while it remained uneven and rough. Often we needed to go up and down through lesser hills. The sub-commissioners, who were in charge after the departure of Ibrahim Effendi, were making an effort to reach Chankiri as soon as possible. The coachmen benefited from the objective of reaching Chankiri at the earliest possible time. They let us out at the bottom of the hills to hasten the journey and give their animals a respite.

Of course we were happy to go on foot like that. Not only did we have a respite from the jolts of the road, which was the biggest of our concerns, we also had opportunity to be together, to talk to each other, to exchange news, to chit-chat, sometimes in amazing light spirits, as if we were not heading to exile.

Soon we received a health bulletin on the sick. Apart from the older Vertanes Papazian, who remained very weak, the rest were in a relatively good condition.

However, Komitas' state had much worsened. He had lost his preoccupation with the gendarmes but had started to obsess about his papers that were left back home in Constantinople. He screamed out of fear and concern for his compositions. To reassure him, they promised him that once we arrived in Chankiri, all necessary arrangements would be made to send for his papers, and he would be able to continue his work in peace. However, they were unable to convince him.

This was the latest manifestation of his nervous condition, which went on all day, especially in the afternoon, when we came close to Chankiri. His situation became acute and disturbing, and it was noticeable to all. They started to talk of his "illness" and express concern that it might have a serious outcome.

Others were surprised about this sudden transformation. From the central jail of Constantinople to Ravli, Komitas did not express any worries. In jail he had preferred to think of developments lightly and held the conviction that things would be corrected soon. He kept himself far from negative and dark thoughts and tried to support others who harbored negative and pessimistic ideas. He tried to help them to overcome hopelessness and anxieties. This was an indication that internally he remained peaceful. This inner peace was what we in general call courage. Among us Komitas was one of the most courageous.

Testimonies are abundant regarding his courage. "He possessed a marvelous physical and mental stamina. He neither needed a bed nor a pillow to sleep the peaceful sleep of a child. He was never foul-mouthed and his speech was happy and taciturn, kind and encouraging to others," wrote Kechian in 1921 (Teotig, *Amenoun Daretsouytsu*, 1922).

The following is the testimony of Dr. Torkomian, written on the occasion of the Varabed's death (*Harach*, 27 October 1935). "...On route to exile I did not want to separate from him. He encouraged not only me but also my friends in exile. He was my strength. ...Without him I had the feeling that enemies were going to take me away. ...He dispersed my fear in such a way that I always wanted to remain in his arms..."

Those who saw him in the above courageous state could not understand the impact of the insignificant incident in Ravli on him. How could the rude act by a gendarme from one moment to the next be capable of destroying his inner peace and transform him in such a way. This remained a riddle in many minds.

The main issue is the following. Was he in inner peace when the incident happened at Ravli? I do not think so.

Komitas, in jail, and throughout the way to exile, remained surrounded by people who from the start were convinced that our arrest was simply a death sentence, and sooner or later all of us would be martyred in this or that place, with this or that excuse, by this or that method. Not all of those who thought this way were martyred. Some were of course among the first survivors, but until then, every day, every hour, they did not talk of anything else. They only obsessed on the inevitable outcome of this ordeal. Among them were historians, such as Kelegian and Kechian, just to mention a few. To give credence to their pessimism, they brought examples of horrors from the French revolution, counting the string of famous heads which the guillotine had harvested. They found similarities, or created similarities, between those severed heads and our own.

Komitas, who of course listened to all these horrible stories repeated over and over again until our arrival at Ravli, had already had his inner peace disturbed. A small incident was enough to precipitate a nervous reaction, as it happened, and even to cause a more serious nervous breakdown. We should not forget that the circumstances around him predisposed him to have a nervous breakdown.

The circumstances were such that the incident with the gendarme was the precipitating factor. But that incident did not disturb anything in him *but revealed something that was already disturbed.* The same thing could have happened even without the incident. Anything else could have triggered it. An ill mannered comment, a poorly thought out gesture, or a joke by any one of us, could have caused a similar reaction.

This could be proven by the fact that eventually *he completely forgot* the gendarmes, who had been such a source of fear for him, while his nervousness continued in a different form.

Another thing that we discovered after we arrived at Chankiri further proved what I said earlier. The reason for the latest obsession about his manuscript was a simple question that was posed by Balakian Vartabed. The latter, who was Komitas' travel mate, simply asked Komitas if he had made any arrangements for the protection of his manuscripts before his arrest.

Komitas remained in the coach throughout the journey. Other lucky people, who were also perched in the *yaylis,* did not come out either. The news was that there were new sick people among them. They named Dr. Torkomian, Father Housig, and Hagop Korian, and this news was not surprising. Torkomian did not sleep all night and was looking after the sick in the khan. The other two were quite elderly gentlemen.

Among the people who were riding the common coaches, Kasbar Cheraz, Mikayel Shamdandjian, Aris Israyelian, Yervant Chavoushian, most probably also others, experienced crises of weakness.

They also did not leave the coaches but the situation of Chavoushian was really unbearable. At each stop he was the first to jump off the coach.

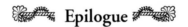 **Epilogue**

Exile, Trauma and Death: On the Road to Chankiri with Komitas Vartabed, 1915 ended abruptly and remained *sharounageli* [to be continued]. However, it was never completed.

Many more chapters would have been needed to wrap up this journey. Volumes two and three of Trilogy-24 will come to add a few more chapters to this unfinished narrative of the Armenian Genocide.

Rita Soulahian Kuyumjian
February 11, 2010

Endnotes

1. The Armenian Question concerned the issue of reforms related to the security of the life and property of Armenians in Ottoman Turkey. The question arose after petitions and demands for reform were made by Armenians who lived in Ottoman Turkey to European Great Powers, asking the latter to pressure the rulers of the Ottoman Empire to introduce reforms. On the one hand these demands became a thorn in the side of Turkish rulers and irritated them to no end. On the other hand, Armenian demands were used by European powers to intervene in Ottoman internal affairs for other purposes. By the 1890s more radical Armenian political parties were formed who proceeded with demands for change. Even the 1908 revolution in the Ottoman Empire proved to be a disappointment. These developments created deep mistrust and animosity between despotic rulers and the Armenian subjects of Ottoman Turkey.

2. Mehmet Talaat Bey was born in 1874. He was one of the leaders of the Committee of Union and Progress, which masterminded the mass murder of Ottoman Armenians in 1915. He was the interior minister, the director of the party's headquarters, and Grand Vezir of the Ottoman Empire (February 1916 to October 1918). During the Armenain Genocide, Talaat reportedly stated that he had done more in three months to solve the Armenian Question than Sultan Hamid did in 30 years. Talaat fled the country two days after the capitulation of the Ottoman Empire in WWI and the Armistice imposed by the Allied Powers. Talaat took refuge in Germany, with the help of Germans, where he wrote his memoirs. He blamed Armenians for their fate and accused them of manipulating European countries against the Ottoman Empire. His memoirs are used by the Turkish nationalists to deny or justify the Armenian Genocide. See Hilmar Kaiser, "From Empire to Republic: The Continuities of Turkish Denial," *Armenian Review,* 2003, vol. 48, no. 3-4, pp. 5-6. Hereafter Hilmar Kaiser.

3. Ismail Enver Pasha (1881-1922). A professional military officer, he was one of the founding members of the Committee of Union and Progress, and one of the masterminds of the Armenian Genocide. In 1909-1911 he was a military attaché in Germany. He was assigned to the post of

Minister of War in 1914. Enver, Talaat Bey and Djemal Bey came to power by force and created the triumvirate that ran the country. He was instrumental in securing a disastrous German-Ottoman alliance. After the defeat of the Ottoman Turks in World War I, he fled to Germany. He was condemned to death in absentia by Ottoman courts in 1919. The charges against him included his role in the Armenian Genocide. He later fled to Central Asia and became the leader of the anti-Soviet Basmaji movement. He died in combat with the Red Army in 1921.

4. Djemal Ahmed Pasha 1872-1922. A leader of the Committee of Union and Progress and one of the more controversial masterminds of the Armenian Genocide. In 1914 he was Minister of Marine. From 1914-18 he was the commander of the Ottoman Fourth Army in Syria. He quashed the defense of Armenians in Ourfa in August 1915. After the defeat of Ottoman Turkey, he took refuge in Germany, where he published his memoirs to justify his actions against Armenians. In 1919 an Ottoman military tribunal condemned him in absentia to death. From 1920-1922 he was a military adviser in Afghanistan. On his way back to Turkey he was assassinated in Tbilisi by two Armenians, Bedros Der Boghosian and Ardashes Kevorkian.

5. Huseyin Cahid Yalçin, *Talaat Pasha*, Istanbul, 1943, p. 63.

6. Soghomon Tehlirian (1886-1960). He was born in Erzerum and died in San Francisco. He served in the army of General Antranik and was injured in action. He assassinated Talaat Pasha in Berlin on 15 March 1921. He was found not guilty by a German jury and was set free.

7. Johaness Lepsius (1858-1926), a clergyman of German origin, a specialist in Eastern languages, he was interested in Armenian issues for many years. He was the president of the German-Armenian Society from 1914-1926. In 1916 he published the book, "Statement on the Condition of Armenians in Turkey," and in 1919, "Germany and Armenia," where he introduced the destruction of Armenians by the Young Turks and the role of Germany in it. In 1921 he bore witness to support Soghomon Tehlirian's defense against Talaat Pasha.

8. All dates have been converted to the Gregorian Calendar.

9. Komitas was a highly respected and cherished Armenian clergyman. He was a musicologist, composer, singer, teacher and choirmaster. He was born in Kutahya, Turkey in 1869 and died in Paris in a mental asylum in 1935. He became a symbol of the Armenian sufferings of 1915. He was elevated in the eyes of many Armenians to martyrdom. His remains were moved to Armenia and are buried in a Pantheon with other Armenian

notables. See Rita Soulahian-Kuyumjian, *Archeology of Madness: Komitas, Portrait of an Armenian Icon,* (Princeton and London, Gomidas Institute), 2001. His six meter bronze statue by the Armenian sculptor Artak Davtian was erected on Place du Canada in Paris as a memorial for the victims of genocides.

10. There were three famous spies who were operating in Constantinople at the time. Artin Mgerdichian, better known as Harun, who was the right hand man of Bedri Bey, the spy who prepared the list of those arrested on April 24, 1915. He also created many problems for Armenian newspapers of Constantinople as a censor. He was injured by an assassin's bullet on March 21, 1919 in Beshiktash (Constantinople) and died 20 days later from his wounds. The other two spies were Arshavir Sahagian and Hmayag Aramyants. The latter had converted to Islam and called himself Hidayet. He was the one who accompanied the Patriarch of Constantinople, Zaven, to his exile. See Teotig, *Amenoun Daretsouytsu, 1916-1920*, p. 180.

11. Zaven Der Yeghiayan, Armenian Patriarch of Constantinople 1913-1922. He wrote his memoirs of those tragic years. Zaven Der Yeghiayan, *My Patriarchal Memoirs*, Mayreni publishing, Princeton, NJ, 2002, Hereafter Zaven Patriarch.

12. The Ayia Sophia Mosque was originally a church in the Byzantine Empire. It was converted into a mosque after the Ottoman conquest of Constantinople.

13. Sarkis Minasian [Aram Ashod] was born in Chenkiler (Yalova) in 1873. He received his education in Bardizag Secondary School and then at Getronagan in Constantinople. He received his higher education in Geneva and lived there until 1903. He often wrote for *Droshak* and went to the United States to become the editor of *Hayrenik* in Boston. He returned to Constantinople in 1909 where he taught and wrote. He became a member of the Armenian National Assembly for Pera, Kasem Pasha. He published critical reviews of lectures given by Armenian physicians. He was a master of the French language and worked on a French-Armenian dictionary. When he was murdered in 1915 the manuscript of his almost finished work was left with his mother. See Teotig, *April 11*, Constantinople, 1919. Reprinted by Government of Armenia Central Committee Press, 1990, p. 34. Hereafter, Teotig.

14. Gigo (Krikor Torosian) was born in Agn in 1884 and was murdered in 1915. He was a comedy writer and published in many Constantinople papers. With Gavrosh, Yervant Odian and Hampigian, they published the

Dzaghig satirical magazine. Then he published his own paper *Gigo* and *Gigoyi Daretsuytse* for five years. Teotig, p. 43.

15. Dr. Dikran Allahverdi survived exile to Chankiri. Zaven Patriarch in his memoirs mentions his name and adds that he never took interest in his nation's life. After his return, he completely withdrew into his shell. See Zaven Patriarch, p. 66.

16. Ibrahim of Izmit. He terrorized the population of Bardizag looking for arms and ammunition. He gathered 300 men and women in the church and viciously beat them. Some guns were found. He gathered the Armenians of Adabazar and threatened to do the same thing with them if they did not hand him weapons. He told them he had orders to do whatever he wanted with them. He added that if they tried to kill him, there would be many more Ibrahims to continue his work. See *Houshamadyan Medz Yegherni* [Memorial to the Greath Calamity], hereafter HMY, p. 506.

17. Bithynia was a region that was settled between the 2nd and 1st centuries BC, east of the Sea of Marmara. By 1915 it had a large Armenian population and included the Monastery of Armash.

18. Ardashes Haroutiunian (Garo) was born in Malgara in 1873. He was a poet and publicist. On 12 August 1915, he was one of the 20 arrested members of the Hunchag party from Samatya (Constantinople) who were brought to jail in Izmit. Ardashes Haroutiunian was badly beaten. He was accused of being a close friend of Hagop Oshagan and knowing the latter's hiding place. He was accused of kidnapping Turkish women during the war with Bulgaria. When his father went to visit his son in jail he was also arrested and imprisoned. Ibrahim of Izmit, after several beatings and tortures, killed both of them on 1 September 1915, outside of Izmit, near Derbend. See HMY p. 314, also Teotig p. 41.

19. Mustafa Reshad (1882-1953) was a high ranking officer who played a significant role in the Armenian Genocide. In 1914 he joined the second department of the political division of Constantinople police and was a member of the council for terrorism. British authorities arrested and kept him in Malta, pending trial, in 1919. One of the charges brought against him was his orchestrated deportation of Armenian intellectuals and political leaders from Constantinople. Under his direction a list of deportees was prepared to include the most active members of the Armenian community. After the arrests he personally interrogated Armenian leaders. He went so far as to dispose of those Armenians acquitted by Ottoman courts. See Hilmar Kaiser.

20. Hagop Djololian was better known as Sirouni. Born in Adabazar in 1890, he died in Bucharest in 1973. He was an Armenologist and a master of Eastern languages. He was arrested in 1908 and 1913 as an undesirable political leader. He lived in hiding in Constantinople from 1915 to 1918, after which he lived in Bucharest. His literary heritage is immense.

21. Hagop Oshagan (Kufedjian). Born in Bursa in 1883 and died in Aleppo in 1948. He was an Armenian writer and literary critic. Among his many works is the multi-volume "Panorama of Western Armenian Literature."

22. Zabel Yesayan, born in Constantinople, 1878, died a victim of Stalin's purges in 1943. She was an Armenian writer, translator, and publicist. She was about to be arrested in the second wave of Armenian intellectuals in Constantinople when she got a visa by her maiden name and was able to escape first to Bulgaria and then to Tbilisi. In 1918 she worked organizing the gathering of Armenian orphans in the Middle East. She was dedicated and supported Soviet Armenia. She was murdered by the KGB in 1943.

23. Shavarsh Misakian. An Armenian writer and editor of *Azadamard,* an ARF newspaper. He survived underground for almost a year before being captured. The arrest of Misakian was the result of an extensive man hunt directed by Mustafa Reshad. See Hilmar Kaiser, p. 11.

24. Diran Kelegian was born in Caesarea (Kayseri) on 20 September 1862. His family moved to Constantinople when he was six months old. He received his grade school education in Haskeoy Nersesian School, then Mesbourian and Sourenian Schools. In 1880 he was sent to Marseille to study commerce and sciences. A student corresponded to *Manzumiye Efkiar,* he was the editor of that paper for 3-4 years. Then he published the Armenian script Turklish language weekly *Djihan.* He became the editorial writer for the paper *Saadet* and then its editor. After the events of 1894 he was obliged to go to Greece and Marseille for political and health reasons. He suffered from a chest disease. After his return he took the editorial responsibility for three papers. During the leadership of Izmirlian Patriarch, he was assigned as the chief translator for the Patriarchate of Constantinople. After the Hamidian massacres he returned to Europe and published articles in *The Nineteenth Century* and *Contemporary Review.* These articles were republished in many European papers. He also wrote in the London *Daily Mail* for the eastern news department for seven months. In 1898 he returned to Constantinople due to an amnesty granted to Ottoman citizens who were in Europe at the time. He corresponded to *Sabah* newspaper. Once more, for political reasons, he had to leave Constantinople for Egypt. He was the editor *Journal de*

Guerre, then chief editor of *La Bourse Egyptienne,* and at the same time corresponded for the Viennese paper *Correspondent Bureau* and the Parisian *Press Associe.* He published *The Egyptian Graphic* for a year, then the Turkish *Yeni Fikir,* the liberal bi-weekly paper for two years. After the declaration the Ottoman constitution he returned to Turkey and was assigned as the chief editor of *Sabah.* He also corresponded to Zohrab's *Masis* periodical, to Shamdandjian's *Dzaghig* and *Masis,* and many other Constantinople Armenian periodicals under many pen names. See Teotig, pp. 26-27.

In 1915, two weeks after his arrival in Chankiri, he was given permission to leave and go anywhere he wanted except to Constantinople. He preferred to stay with other exiles, although he dreamed of taking refuge at a seashore. He knew the policies of the Ittihadists very well. He used to say that they were going to implement the Armenian massacres with mathematical accuracy. Kelegain had received news from his wife in Constantinople that the German ambassador Wangenheim asked after his safety. The day after Wangenheim's death in October, 1915, Kelegian was arrested and ostensibly taken to a military tribunal in Chorum. He asked one of the clergymen to say prayers for his soul. He was killed soon afterwards. See Mikayel Shamdandjian in Teotig, pp. 137-8.

25. Dr. Stepan Miskdjian was born in Constantinople in 1852. Graduating in medicine in Germany, he specialized in obstetrics and gynaecology. He was a member of his local Catholic church council in Ortakeoy. His brother, a 50 year-old pharmacist, was also arrested and killed in exile. See Teotig, p. 55.

26. Krikoris Vartabed Balakian was arrested and exiled to Chankiri. He survived the Genocide with the help of German officers and later worked as the Bishop of the Armenian church in Manchester (England). He was one of the witnesses at the trial of Talaat Pasha's assassin in Berlin, 1921. Balakian wrote the two volume work, *The Armenian Golgotha, Episodes from Armenian Martyrdom: From Berlin to Der Zor, 1914- 1920.*

27. Zaven Der Yeghiayan, Armenian Patriarch of Constantinople, 1913-1922. In his memoirs Zaven Patriarch mentions that after his election as Patriarch he had tried to assign prelacy Vicars to important prelacies in the Ottoman provinces that did not have Prelates. He wanted to assign prelates who were knowledgeable in languages and had political savvy. Father Krikoris Balakian had just returned from his studies in Germany and was offered the position of the Vicar of Yerzinga [Erzinjan], but he refused the assignment. Zaven Patriarch mentions that he did not put any pressure on Father Balakian as the latter mentions in his book, *The*

Armenian Golghota. Instead Sahag Vartabed Odabashian accepted the assignment and was brutally murdered on his way to his post. See Zaven Patriarch, pp. 54-5.

28. Agnouni (Khachadour Malouomian), was born in Meghri. He was approximately 50 years old when he started to write in *Mshag* (Tbilisi). He lived in St. Petersburg for a long time and wrote for *Droshak,* the official organ of the ARF, mainly about the Russian government's attitude toward the Caucasus and Russian Armenians. He published his articles under "Caucasian News" section. He wrote on the Armenian-Tatar clashes under the headlines of "Caucasian Wounds" which he later published and translated to French. He participated in the Young Turks' and Armenians' conference in Paris in 1904. In 1907 he was elected by the ARF conference as a delegate and played an important role in the reintroduction of the Ottoman Constitution after 1908. His public appearances in Constantinople met with great enthusiasm. In 1912 he left for the United States, visited Armenian communities, and returned to Constatinople. Then he published an essay on Krikor Ardzrouni. He was the author of "Tebi Griv" [To the Fight], "Tebi Yergir" [To the Fatherland] and "Medz Idialiste" [The Great Idealist]. He was one of the unsigned editorial writers of *Azadamrd* daily in Constantinople. See Teotig, p. 25.

29. Khajag K. (Karekin Chakalian). Born in Alexandropol, 1867 and murdered in 1915. He studied at the Kevorkian Seminary. He studied Social Sciences at the University of Geneva. He was imprisoned for eight years for his political activities. He was freed and worked as a teacher in Shushi, Karabagh. In 1908 he was arrested again and freed, only to be arrested and kept in jail in the infamous Medekh prison in Tbilisi, in Baku, Rosdov and Novochersk. In 1912 he came to Constantinople and was assigned as the director of Samatia National School. He was a famous teacher, involved in national affairs, and a publicist. He was a good orator. According to him, he inherited his ability from his mother, Mrs. Sultan. He published many works. He translated three volume of Vinogradov's work, "General History of Nations." See HMY, p. 517, also Teotig, p. 23. At the end of the entry in Teotig, there is a hurriedly written letter from Khajag from exile to his wife: "My dear, they are taking me far, far away from you to Dikranagerd. The following friends from Ayash are with me: Agnouni, Zartar, Sarkis Minasian, Doctor Dagahavarian and Djihangul. At the Ereyli station I met an Armenian who promised to bring this letter to you. Take good care of yourself and my daughters, Nunus and Alos. We do not know why they are taking us there. But I have great hopes that we

will see each other again. For now, goodbye, I kiss you and our children. Yours, K. Khajag. May 1915.

30. Siamanto (Adom Yardjanian) was born in Agn in 1878. At the age of 13 he moved to Constantinople and attended Mirijanian and Berberian schools. He actively started to participate in Armenian national and literary life. The diaspora papers opened their pages to his mastery epic writing. He returned to Constantinople at the end of 1908 and wrote for *Azadamard*. Among his published works are a series called "Hayortinere" [Sons and Daughters of the Armenian Nation], "Hokevarki yev Houysi Chaher" [Torches of Agony and Hope], "Garmir Lourer Paregames" [Red News from My Friend] on the Cilician massacres, all of which were published in a complete anthology in the United States. Some of his works were translated into English. Siamanto will live in Armenian Literature as the unparalleled master of *khorhertabashd* (symbolic) poetry. See Teotig, p. 28.

31. Adom (Haroutiun Shahrigian) was born in Shabin Karahisar in 1860 and was murdered in 1915. He was a lawyer, teacher, and a member of the Armenian National Assembly. His most important works were "Bedagan Norokoutiounn ou Hoghayin Hartse" [The Government Reforms and the Land Question], "Azkayin Sahmanatroutiune" [The National Constitution], "Parenorokoumnerou Hartse" [The Issue of Reforms] and others. See HMY p. 517.

32. Roupen Zartarian was born in Severeg in western Armenia in 1874. His family moved to Kharpert. He was a student of Tlgadentsi. He was arrested for political activities in 1903-04 at the age of 21. He moved to Bulgaria in 1905 and lived in Plovdiv and published the periodical *Razmig* until the declaration of the Ottoman Constitution in 1908. After the Young Turk revolution he returned to Constantinople. In 1910 he published his free prose in *Tsaykaluys*. He was famed as a master writer of free prose. He also published a series of school books, *Meghraked*. He was a dedicated and firm believer in the Armenain Revolutionary Federation. After his return to Constantinople on June 9, 1910, he established the newspaper *Azadamard*. Until his exile, he was the chief editor and ran the paper with competence. Many able writers corresponded for the paper. He wrote unsigned fiery, politically savvy editorials. He lectured at many party meetings and was elected a member of the Armenian National Assembly. He was murdered in 1915. Teotig, p. 32.

33. Hratch (Hayg Tiryakian). Born in Trabizon in 1871. He studied agriculture in Nancy, France. He became a famous revolutionary when he participated in the siege of the Ottoman Bank in Constantinople. He was

freed and was transferred to Marseille with his friends. He returned secretly to Smyrna and was arrested and given a life sentence to serve in Bodrum. After the declaration of the 1908 Constitution, he was freed and returned to Constantinople. He became the next publisher of *Azadamrd* and published many important books. He also had a personal business and supplied materials to the Ministry of War. He was murdered in 1915. See Teotig, p. 53.

34. Marzbed (Ghazar Ghazarian). Born in Tamzara in 1878, he was orphaned at a young age and brought to Constantinople where he attended Bezjian School. His uncle sent him to Munich where he specialized in education. He went to Bulgaria and worked as a teacher. The ARF sent him to Persia as its representative in Khoy. He presented himself to the Persian government as a deputy to the church vicar. He participated in the Armenian-Tatar war and organized the transport of ammunition. After the declaration of the Constitution in Turkey, he returned and engaged in teaching in Paghesh (Bitlis) and mingled with all classes of the population. He taught in Constantinople and went into hiding during the 1915 arrests. He came out of hiding to help a newly arrested friend and was arrested himself. He was exiled in Caesarea and he succeeded in convincing the Major in charge to let him come to Constantinople to engage in pro-Turkish propaganda for the Caucasus. Few days later he was arrested once more and exiled. His life was dedicated to being a revolutionary and an intellectual. He was murdered in 1915. See Teotig, p. 50.

35. Shavarsh Krisian was born in Beshigtash on July 9, 1886. He attended the American College in Bardizag, and Berberian and Robert College in Uskudar. In 1906 he went to Paris and studied physical education in Lycee Janson in Debone and then studied in London for two and a half years. He graduated and returned to Constantinople and was assigned and taught physical education in different schools of Constantinople. He also organized sports clubs in different suburbs of the city. In 1911 he published *Marmnamarz* (The Coach) monthly which lasted four years and helped to educate the public on physical health matters. He published the book "The Boy Scout, and the Purpose of His Life." He was an ARF member and a brother of Doctor Djanig Krisian. See Teotig, p. 46. His name was inscribed on the walls of Ayash prison. In Ayash jail he organized the inmates to exercise and not lose their strength. The guards thought that this was military training and forbade the inmates to do the exercises. See Teotig, p. 122.

36. Parsegh Shahbaz was born in Boyajikeoy (on the Bosphorus) in June 1883. He graduated from Getronagan in Constantinople and finished his education in Venice at Mkhitarian School. He enrolled in the ranks of the ARF by Avedis Aharonian. In Constantinople he published *Dzaghig* (Flower) paper with Mikayel Shamdandjian. He fled to Egypt after an assassination attempt on Patriarch Ormanian in Constantinople. He continued his public life and returned to Constantinople just before the declaration of the 1908 Constitution and traveled to the provinces to do public work. He went to Paris in 1912 to study law. He returned to Constantinople before the war for duty assigned to him by Victor Berar. He was endowed with a double gift: rhetorical speaking and beautiful writing skills. Teotig, p. 40.

37. Hrant (Melkon Gurdjian). Born in September 1859 in Havou (Palou). Immigrating to Constantinople in 1870, he attended Uskudar Gymnasium until 1875, having Mihran Tourian (later Bishop Yeghishe Tourian) as a classmate. He then went to Sourp Khatch – K. Misakian's classes. From 1878 until 1896 he untiringly taught Classical Armenian and literature in various schools (Rodosto, the Getronagan School in Galata, Samatia's Nounian-Vartouhian, Mezbourian and so on). He escaped to Varna during the troubles of 1896, where he opened, in partnership with Miss A. Minasian, the Ardzrounian School, named in memory of K. Ardzrouni, whom he admired. When he returned to Constantinople in 1898 he was thrown into prison and, six months later, was exiled to Kastamouni, where he lived for ten years, working as a teacher. He contributed articles to the Armenian newspapers (*Masis, Arevelk, Hairenik*) of Constantinople continuously from 1883 concerning language and community politics, of which the series "The Life Of An Immigrant" will always be remembered with its pictures, life and trembling distress. In his life of exile – when he was forbidden books and writing materials – he diffidently produced, in his marshy banishment, the large novel of family life on two axes, which began to be serialised, without signature, in *Sourhantag* and which suddenly ceased after 18 parts... as a result of censorship. Hrant was matched against authoritative people (Berberian and Tourian) concerning Classical Armenian on three occasions and demonstrated his great expertise. During his time in Varna, he contributed articles, under the nom-de-plume "Shavasp" to the paper *Sharjoum*. When he returned to Constantinople with the proclamation of the Ottoman Constitution, he enthusiastically embraced teaching, without neglecting his literary work. He was a community assembly deputy. He was a Tashnag. He was the author of a Classical Armenian

textbook, a history of Armenian letters with the title of *Mesrob Yev Sahag* [Mesrob and Sahag], as well as a translation of *Inch Ge Khorhin Ginere Irents Amousinnerou Masin?* [What Do Women Think About Their Husbands?]. He was murdered in 1915.

38. Taniel Varoujan (Taniel Chiboukiarian) was born on April 20, 1884 in Sepastia (Sivas), western Armenia, to Armenian Catholic parents and was murdered on August 26, 1915 with Roupen Sevag, a doctor, and three other friends in Tuney Khan, outside of Chankiri where he was exiled. He was an ARF member. He is considered one of the most gifted western Armenian poets ever. He received his high school education in Venice's Mourad Raphaelian School, and university education in Ghent, Belgium. He taught a wide variety of subjects in different Armenian schools. Between 1912 and 1915 he was the director of Lusavorich School in Constantinople. He had plans to create an Armenian Writers' Society, by the name of "Asdghadun." He published *Navasart* yearbook. He also participated in the publication of *Mehyan* literary magazine. His most revered works are "Sarsourner" [Shivers], "Tseghin Sirde" [The Heart of the Race], "Hetanos Yerker" [Pagan Songs], "Hatsin Yerke" [Song of the Bread]. His poetry on love, human suffering and patriotism were beuatiful. He was a prolific poet.. See Teotig, pp. 30, 136. On 8 February 1958, in Ghent, an evening dedicated to Varoujan was organized by his alma-mater and a commemorative plaque was placed in the hall of the university. In Yerevan a street and a school were named after him.

39. Aris Israyelian (Israyel Dkhrouni) was born in Gumushhane in 1885. He was a graduate of Mourad Raphaelian School in Venice. He studied agriculture in the United States and enrolled in the ranks of the ARF. He wrote political articles in *Hayrenik* in Boston, where he published a study on Armenian immigration to the United States. In 1910 he returned to Constantinople. He taught, wrote in *Azadamard,* and did lobbying work for the party. See Teotig, p. 47.

40. Dr. Garabed Khan Pashayan, was born in Gedig Pasha in 1864. He graduated from medical school in Constantinople and worked as a family doctor in Palu and Malatya. In 1889 he settled in Gevrig where he continued to work as a doctor. The following year he was arrested for organizing revolutionary groups and was given a death sentence. He was granted amnesty for his death sentence by the judge whose eyes he cured. Then he was arrested once more, and after spending three years in different jails, he once more was given the death sentence. With the intervention of the British consul in Constantinople, he was pardoned once again. He went to Persia and lived in Tabriz for seven years. He

became the doctor of the Shah but did not stop doing benevolent work. In 1903-06 he opened a publishing house in Alexandria, Egypt and published *Horizon* newspaper. He was invited back to Persia and lived in the city of Bender Gez earning titles and awards. After the declaration of the constitution he returned to Constantinople and became a member of the Armenian National Assembly for Kharput. He is the author of more than two dozen literary and scientific works in French. See Teotig, p. 37.

41. Hampartsoum Hampartsoumian was born in Constantinople in 1890. He graduated from Yesayan and Getronagan Schools. He published his first article in *Surhantag* and then in *Azadamard,* writing articles on economics and legislative subjects. He corresponded to *La Turquie, Levant Herald, Tageblat, Kölnische* Zeitung, and *Humanite.* He was a member of the ARF. See Teotig, p. 39.

42. Nerses Papazian. Born in Akoulis (in the Caucasus) in 1872, the son of the priest Rev Mesrob "Shoushdag", and brother of the well-known writer Vertanes and of Vahan. Moving to Van, after spending his childhood there he came to Constantinople and was a student in Yedikouleh orphanage. He then went to Armash and, completing the necessary training, was ordained a celibate priest, being re-christened Rev Mashtots; he and his six classmates were the first graduates of the Armash seminary. He was sent to the USA as a pastor where he worked with Bishop Saradjian. Then he graduated from Columbia University in New York. He became a Tashnag party member. After serving as pastor in the USA for nine years, he went to the Caucasus and participated in the Armeno-Tatar disturbances. For speaking out on the occasion of the enforced take-over of Armenian Church property, the Russian government demanded his banishment from Etchmiadzin. Rev. Mashtots was appointed prelate of Tehran, where he remained for two years. He was forced to renounce his church calling, as he was a community activist, and went to the USA, taking over the editorship of *Hairenik* at the end of 1906, in place of Vramian. After the Constitution was proclaimed he came to Constantinople and travelled through the nearby provinces as a propagandist. When *Azadamard* was published, he became the permanent editor of the Armenian section until April 11th 1915. The articles in the paper describing crimes that had been committed flowed from his pen. He was one of the founders of the "Ashkhadanki Doun" and a teacher in the "Arti Varjaran". Towards the end he attempted to become a lawyer in marriage cases before the courts, as a person well versed in Church law. Teotig, pp. 54-5.

43. Kegham Parsegian was born in Constantinople in 1883. He received his primary education in Gedig Pasha National School at the same time as Vartkes (Serengulian) and Levon Shant. At a young age he liked to work for newspapers and did his debut at the *Manzume* publishing house. He also was a permanent editor in *Azadamard*. A close friend of Shavarsh Misakian on 16 December 1908 he published *Aztag* literary magazine. In total he published 41 issues. Later he published *Mehyan* with Gosdan Zarian and Hagop Kufedjian. He was a promising talent. He was a member of the ARF. See Teotig, p. 44.

44. Sarkis Svin (Sarkis Sungudjian) was born in Beshigtash in Constatinople in 1870. He was a graduate of Mulkie School. He was a functionary in the Ottoman government from 1892-1896. He was arrested on 1 June, 1896, accused of working as a mediator between Patriarch Izmirlian and foreign reporters. After spending seven months in jail, he benefited from a general amnesty and fled to Egypt, then to Bulgaria, where he taught and worked as a businessman. He corresponded for two years to *Iravunk* [Rights] under the signature S.S. After the declaration of the Ottoman Constitution he returned to Constantinople and was elected as a member of the Armenian National Assembly from Kum Kapu and was sent to Adana as a delegate after the Adana Massacres. He was a member of the Assembly's Political Committee, as well as a member of the Investigative Committee of the Patriarchate and the Committee for the Care of the Orphans. See Teotig, pp. 52-3.

45. (Jirayr) Partogh Zorian. Born in Tamzara on the 1st of January 1879 and received his primary education there, continuing it in Yerzinga. Going to Filipe when he was 18, he continued special courses there. He was a Dashnak. When R. Zartarian began to publish "Razmig" there, Partogh looked after its administration. Coming to Constantinople at the proclamation of the Constitution, he founded the "Lousaghpiur" publishing house with Onnig Srabian (Onnig-Jirayr), producing the "Meghraked" series, "Hoghakordzin Paregame" and so on. He was elected Armenian National Assembly deputy from Shabin Karahissar. See Teotig, p. 63.

46. Yenovk Shahen was born in Bardizag in 1881. He was the brother of the mathematician Krikor Ankut, who survived the Genocide. He was an actor. He played Yago in Shakespear's Otello, Shylok in the Merchant of Venice, and Hugo's Tribule. He was a member of the ARF. He was killed in Ayash, 1915. See Teotig, p. 54.

47. Krikor Ankout was a mathematician who survived the Genocide. See Teotig, p. 54.

48. Mihrtad Haygazn. Born in Beshiktash in 1864. He graduated from the Makrouhian School there. In 1883 he became involved in revolutionary life, resulting in his being exiled to Tripoli by N. Melhameh. Returning to Constantinople at the proclamation of the Constitution, he had his misfortunes and the ways his persecutors operated staged as a play. He went to Etchmiadzin three times as a delegate at the election of Izmirlian and subsequent catholicoses. He held many community positions, to the point that he neglected his umbrella selling trade. He was elected community assembly deputy from Rodosto. He was the chairman of the Beshiktash "Aharonian Club". See Teotig, p. 59.

49. Mourad (Hampartsoum Boyadjian). Born in Hadjin in 1867. After receiving his primary education in the local Miatsial School, he came to Constantinople and, receiving his diploma from the Idad School, he entered the Medical University, which he was forced to leave before he graduated. He was the first organiser, in 1888, of the Hunchagian party. As a result of his virulent opposition to the Hamid regime and main organiser of the Kum Kapu "unarmed protest", he was forced to escape to Athens. He went from the Caucasus to Sassoun at the order of the party centre, to lead the 1895 rebellion that finally gave the European powers the opportunity to intervene and put forward the May 11th Reform Plan. He was regarded as the saviour of the population of the Sassoun region, as he was able to live, preserving his life, possessions and honour for some time. It was during that rebellion that Mourad was arrested and thrown into Paghesh prison, where he spent two years. He was tried and sentenced to death that, thanks to foreign intervention, was reduced to life imprisonment. After spending 12 years imprisoned in Tripoli, he was able to escape in 1904 and went to France. After spending some time there, he went to the New World, being the object of enthusiastic demonstrations by Armenians there. Returning to Constantinople just before the proclamation of the Constitution, he was elected the community assembly deputy from Kum Kapu and *mebous* from Adana. He opposed the army conscription of non-Muslims, as well as the extension of the Sultan's authority in the parliament. He spoke vehemently about the Cilician disaster, gaining the enmity of his Turkish fellow-parliamentarians. He was a member of the Political Assembly. He was Dr. Djelal's brother-in-law. He was also immortal Jirayr's brother, who had been hanged in the name of Armenian emancipation during the time of the old tyranny, and like whom he too would become immortal, years later – on 24th August 1915 - putting the final full stop to his Armenian race's martyrdom as the

rope was put around his neck, like so many sons of Armenia who yearned for freedom. See Teotig, pp. 48-9.

50. Doctor Krikor Djelal was the husband of Mourad's sister.

51. Ardzrouni (Hagop Avedisian). Born in Van in 1873. Coming to Constantinople when he was 17, he joined the Hntchagian party. He escaped to Bulgaria at the time of the Baab Ali demonstration and was convicted and sentenced to death in his absence. After wandering through Athens, Egypt and the Caucasus for a number of years, he was thrown into Medekh prison in Tiflis. At the end of 1898 he went to Van and, in 1903, when the wounded Vartkes was arrested there, he was imprisoned again on the assumption that he was his fellow-activist. The next year he went to Persia and became a teacher. He came to Constantinople at the proclamation of the Constitution, to carry out party work and was elected community assembly deputy from Gedik Pasha and a member of the "Vanoreits Khorhourt". He contributed to various Constantinople papers and others abroad. See Teotig, page 55.

52. Hagter (Hagop Terzian). Born in Hadjin on 22 August 1879, and received his primary education there, then in the Adana community and Jesuit schools. He came to Constantinople in 1897. He received his diploma in pharmacology in 1900. He ran pharmacies successively in Hadjin and Adana, at the same time sending articles to the newspapers in Constantinople under the nom-de-plumes of "Hagter", "Hmayag", "Davros", "Hito" and "Tghtagits". He only just escaped the disaster in Cilicia and returned to Constantinople, where he opened the "Adana" pharmacy in Kum Kapu. He was the author of *Arvest Lousangarchoutian* and *Adanayi Gianke Yev Giligio Aghede* (5 volumes). The latter book was presented to Izmiriantz. It was confiscated in toto by the government.

53. Haroutiun G. Djangulian. Born in Van in 1855. He was an early Hntchag activist. He came to Constantinople in 1881and, in 1890, as a result of his extreme boldness and actual participation in the Kum Kapu "unarmed demonstration", was arrested and suffered dreadful torture, and was sentenced to death. He managed to escape, however, and go abroad, always remaining faithful to his oath, until the Constitution was proclaimed. Returning to Constantinople, he was elected the community assembly deputy from Gedik Pasha, as well as a member of the founding assembly of the "Miatsial Ungeroutiun". His *Hishadagner Haygagan Djuknazhamen*, in four volumes, contained the events and personalities from national revolutionary life, with noteworthy documents as sources for our modern history. See Teotig, p. 51.

54. Sako. An Armenian from the Caucasus who was a well-known personality in the Hntchagian party. He studied rural economy in Paris, during which time he established relations with Nazar Beg and others. During the 1895 Sassoun rebellion, it was he who provided all possible help, both financial and moral, to the hero Mourad (H. Boyadjian) as speedily as possible. He participated many times in the affairs of the Hntchagian Caucasian committee and was a member of the editorial staff of the newspaper *Kaghapar*. Being one of the organisers of the terror act against Golitzin, the Russian government exiled him to Siberia. He came to Constantinople after the proclamation of the Constitution, where he stayed until his deportation. He was killed in Ayash. See, Teotig, p. 56.

55. Dr. Nazaret Daghavarian. (Adapted from his extensive, unpublished autobiography.) I was born in Sepastia on 25th December 1862. Coming to Constantinople at seven years old, I attended the Amenaprgchian School, which I graduated from in 1878, then going to France. After a year on farms familiarising myself with agriculture, I attended the agricultural school at Meurce and, after graduating in 1881, won a scholarship to the Agricultural School in Paris and graduated, two years later, with the title of agricultural engineer. It was at that time too that I was a student at the schools of dendrology and viticulture. Returning to Constantinople in 1883, and after working for some months in the Ministry of Agriculture, I was appointed the director on the school in my birthplace, establishing a lecture hall, a Sunday school for mature people and sending articles to the newspapers in Constantinople. I was the director of the Aramian School in Kadekiugh in 1885-1886. At the beginning of 1887, going to Paris, I attended lessons at the Sorbonne and the Medical School, continuing the publication of "Kidagan Sharjoum" I had begun in Constantinople in 1885. Having received my diplomas, I came to live in Pera. I became an assistant doctor in the French Hospital in 1987, and the chief doctor in the Armenian community hospital in 1899. It was the troubled period of the Hamid regime; they searched my house and questioned me many times. In 1896 I went to prison and was released four months later in the general pardon. I once more went to prison in 1900, but the French ambassador had me freed. I gave medical lectures in the hospital to students of all nationalities, with the object of giving them practical training. The police, regarding this as evil, forbade me to visit the hospital. The surveillance hadn't stopped; I decided to leave the country and, while making my preparations, heard that I was being sought... I obtained refuge as a patient in the French Hospital, which was surrounded and from which I was only able to escape to Marseilles four

months later. I settled in Cairo at the end of 1905. I gave the community educational effort some help and, with a few friends and under the patronage of Boghos Pasha founded the "Armenian General Benevolent Union", whose secretary and administrator I was until the time I left Egypt. With the proclamation of the Constitution, I returned to Constantinople with my family and was elected a community assembly deputy, then *mebous* for Sepastia when I was in the Caucasus for the election of the Catholicos. As a fervent nationalist, I had arguments mainly about the land question and in defence of community rights. Until the end I was against my Armenian friends, and was the founder of "Itilaf". Offices I've held: Inspector of the community hospital (1895), member of the Teachers Inspection Committee (1895-1897), Trustee of the Pera schools (1894-1896), member of the Political Assembly (1910-1912) and Izmiriantz (1912-1915). Assistant (1912) then Municipal General Inspector (1913). My works: *Pnagan Badmoutiun, Ousoumnasiroutiun Mizayin Karerou Yev Ayln* (in French), *Dzakoumn Hai Darits, Manreyapanoutiun* (also in Turkish), *Diezerk Yev ir Gazmoutiun* (also in French), *Krikor Aghaton, Ardnin Aroghchabhoutiun, Dznentagan Kordzarank, Martgayin Sagemakhosoutiun, Paratsoutsag Akhdanvants, Darvinaganoutiun, Hayots Hin Gronkneru, Martgayin Gazmakhosoutiun, Aroghchabahoutiun, Ourvakidz Badmoutian Hayots, Manerk. Poghokaganoutiun* and a few booklets. From my unpublished work I'll just recall a book that I started in 1886 and finished 18 years later – a ten volume *Gentanapoudzoutiun* I prepared at Izmirlian's urging. My nom-de-plumes are "Ararchahiut", "Poragadzin", "Diun", "***", "Sgsnag Panaser" and "SP".

The historian-doctor, with much to his credit, modestly passes over the fact that in 1902 the French government granted him the title *Officier d'Academie*, and in 1910 he received the *Merite Agricole* medal.

56. Dr. Khachig Boghosian survived the Genocide. See "My Arrest and Exile" in *The Armenian Reporter*, translated by Aris Sevag, April 21, 2001.

57. Mikayel Shamdandjian survived Chankiri and lived to write his memoirs about his friends of Chankiri. He was asked by Teotig to draw a picture of life in Chankiri in those days of horror. He explained that some thirty of them, from a total of 150 people, were allowed to return to Constantinople from Chankiri. Out of the remaining 120, barely 15 survived. The remaining 100 were killed under most horrendous circumstances. They were divided into two caravans: the first consisted of 52 and the second of 24 exiles. Both were directed toward Der Zor. From the first, only the bookseller Baronian, who was a Protestant, survived.

From the second caravan, Aram Andonian, who broke his leg when he fell off a carriage, was left in a hospital in Angora. They could not make him walk. The remaining people in the caravan were taken on foot three hours away from Angora and killed at the foot of Elma Mountain. The way that the caravans were formed was mostly decided locally. It was left at the discretion of the local functionaries and local Ittihad party members. Very little instructions came from the center. Mikayel Shamdandjian's name was on the list of the first caravan but because of the similarity of his name with someone else, he was left behind by sheer luck. The second caravan was formed of people who earned their living in the city doing useful jobs. The responsibility of these lists and the caravans fell on the Ittihadist party secretary Oghuz, who was responsible for the death of 100 people. Three of the victims who were close to Shamdandjian were Varoujan, Sevag and Kelegian. Shamdandjian left Chankiri with seven friends after the arrest of Kelegian. The remaining 20 were taken away with the Armenians of Kastemuni and only three survived. The remaining died under difficult circumstances and epidemics. Teotig, p. 131-9. Mikayel Shamdandjian translated to Armenian from its original German Doctor Lepsius' work "The Secret Report on the Massacres in Armenia".

58. Piuzant Bozadjian survived Ayash. He was Teotig's first cousin. He wrote his memoirs of Ayash in Teotig. "To Ayash: Old and New Memoirs". The article describes the circumstances of his arrest, life in the jail at Ayash, a proposal from the Ittihad, the birthday of the National Constitution, Sultan Reshad's birthday, and finally, the circumstances of his freedom. See Teotig, pp. 113-30.

59. Vramshabuh was born in Samatia in 1880. He was a businessmen and a volunteer in different Armenian organizations. He was a member of the committee after the Adana massacres to organize help for orphans and widows. See Teotig, p. 60.

60. Hagop Nargiledjian a pharmacist. He was one of the eight people who were freed from Chankiri with Komitas. See Ahmet Altintas et al, eds., *Osmanli Belgelerinde Ermeniler* [Armenians in Ottoman Documents] (1915-1920), Ankara, Prime Ministry Archives, 1994.

61. R. Sevag (Dr. Roupen Chilingirian). Born in Silivri on 15th February 1885. Having received his primary education there, he went to Bardizag, then to the Berberian school, graduating from there in 1905. Apart from his talent as a writer, having a great bent for science, he went to Lausanne on the advice of his school's principal and with a bursary and, hardly having completed medical school and received his diploma, practiced in hospitals and dispensaries, also gaining experience in the art of mysteries.

The dreamer and scientist both lived in him. He couldn't forsake the lyre for the sake of Hippocrates, and sang of humanity, the fatherland and love. In 1910 he published *Garmir Kirku*, having been affected by the massacres in Cilicia. His great poem "Verchin Hayere" seems like a prophesy of final Armenian martyrdom, while his best work – as poetry – is "Lemani Lidje". In 1914 he came and settled with his German wife in Pera, Constantinople, to continue his work as a doctor. He began writing a series of articles in *Azadamard* under the title "Pjishkin Kirken Prtsvads Echer" that were read with great enthusiasm by everyone. Just before the outbreak of the war, when the Armenian doctors began a course in nursing as a body, Sevag received applause for his captivating and useful lectures. It was when he was serving as a doctor in the Makrikez Division of the Turkish Army that he was separately deported to Chankiri. See Teotig p. 32.

62. Rev. Keropian was one of the eight who was freed with Komitas, his name was in the telegram cited above. Ahmet Altintas et al, eds., Osmanli Belgelerinde Ermeniler [The Armenians in Ottoman Documents] (1915-1920) (Ankara, Basbakanlik,1994), p. 26.

63. Doctor Vahram Torkomian. Born in Constantinople, 1858. He was a medical doctor. Arrested on 24 April 1915, he was also one of the lucky prisoners who were released from Chankiri, along with Komitas.

64. Arisdages Kasbarian. Born in Adana in 1861, a lawyer who practiced in Constantinople. He was elected a member of the National Assembly from Adana. He participated in many committees. He authored important articles in *Manzoumiye, Piuzantion, Surhantag* on controversial social issues. All his works were legal and written in Turkish, many of which were republished several times. Teotig p. 50.

65. Piuzant Kechian was one of the eight people who survived Chankiri and returned to Constantinople. He was the editor of *Piuzantion* which was published from 1896-1918. It was a political, literary and scientific paper. Aram Andonian reflects a great deal on Kechian throughout the articles. Zaven Patriarch writes the following in his memoirs about Kechian. "Piuzant Kechian returned to Constantinople on 1 May 1915 and found a chance to go to Bulgaria a short time later. He stayed in Filipe [Plovdiv] until the end of the war. Upon his return from Chankgiri, Kechian immediately declared that the [Echmiadzin] Catholicos' name should no longer be mentioned in our churches. He defended this thesis in the weekly *Dajar*, which was published after my deportation by Hrant Vartabed Hovasapian and Haroutiun Mugurdichian... When Kamer Shirinian went to see his children in Filipe in January 1916, Kechian told

him, 'Everybody other than the Patriarch can accept Islam in order to save themselves.' I do not know how Kechian succeeded in coming back from exile and how he received permission to leave for Bulgaria. I found it quite amazing." The Patriarch went on to state that Piuzant Kechian had received permission to go to Filipe after his return from exile and was registered on the government's list of spies. After arriving in Filipe, he had always sent his reports to the Constantinople police, signing them as "Kadri". Dr. Avedis Nakkashian in 1937 published an article in *Hayeli ashkharhi* [Mirror to the world], published in Bulgaria, where he confirms that Piuzant Kechian was a spy and that that fact was well known to the Armenians of Filipe. Zaven Der Yeghiayan, Armenian Patriarch of Constantinople, 1913-1922. "My patriarchal memoirs" was published in English translation in April 2002, Princeton NJ, p. 66. The editors of the Patriarch's book added an endnote that "After the Armistice, Hrant Vartabed immediately abandoned the cowl and left Constantinople for America, where he made himself forgotten. The traitor Haroutiun Mugurdichian confined himself to his house, but he met his just punishment through an Armenian's bullet, which found him sitting by the window."

66. Serovpe Noradoungian was born in Sghert in 1884. He graduated from Sanasarian School. From 1903-05 he taught Turkish. He followed university courses in the Ottoman University. He was elected a member of the Armenian National Assembly from Sghert. He was an ARF member. See Teotig, p. 57.

67. Apig Djambaz, Catholic Armenian from Pera. See Teotig, p. 62.

68. The Vatican protested the massacre of Armenians and sought special protection for Catholic Armenians. Pope Benedict the XV wrote a letter to the Sultan demanding to spare Catholic Armenians. The letter arrived in September. By then most Catholic Armenians were deported with other Armenians. John F. Pollard, *The Unknown Pope: Benedict XV (1912-1922) and the Pursuit of Peace*, London: Geoffrey Chapman, 1999. Teotig lists the names of 40 Catholic clergy and Catholic sisters who were killed. See Teotig p. 106-111. Teotig collected this information from Mkhitarist Father, Hovsep Der Markarian's Complete Obituary manuscript. *Ibid* p. 106. Zaven Patriarch in his memoirs mentions that Msgr. Dolci asked the Patriarch to write a letter to the Pope at the beginning of February 1916, requesting the Pope's intervention on behalf of Armenians. See Zaven Patriarch, pp. 101-102.

69. Many Armenians converted to Protestantism starting in 1831 when American and European missionaries went to work in the Ottoman

Empire. By the end of the century the American Board of Commissioners for Foreign Missions (ABCFM) had twelve stations and 270 outstations in Asiatic Turkey. About 150 missionaries and 114 organized churches made more than thirteen thousand Armenian converts to Protestantism. The missionaries taught over sixty thousand students in their 132 high schools and 1100 elementary schools, and ran six colleges and various theological seminaries. Suzanne E. Moranian, "The American Missionaries and the Armenian Question, 1915-1920", Ph.D dissertation, University of Wisconsin-Madison, 1994, p. 52.

70. Mutasaref Asaf Bey became a scapegoat and lost his position for five years after the Adana massacres of 1909. He had just been assigned as mutasarif to Chankiri when he was transferred elsewhere due to his kind regard towards Armenians.

71. Onnig Maghazajian was born in Constantinople in 1878. He was the owner of a bookbinding business called "Vatan." He published huge maps of Ottoman Turkey, as well as a pocket atlas. He was the president of Kum Kapu "Harachatimaser Ungeroutiune" [The Progressive Society] for which he was exiled.

72. Der-Ghazarentz (Smpad Purad). Born in Zeitoun on 3rd March 1862. He studied in the seminary in Jerusalem from 1871-1880. a post as teacher and school director. He was in Zeitoun from 1882-1884 as a teacher in the Miatsial School. It was at that time that he was a colleague of K. Dadourian, with whom he produced the *Ulnia* or *Zeitouni Deghakraganu.* H Allahverdian, who later published it as his own work, filched this document, in its manuscript form. He opened a school in Sis in 1885. Coming to Constantinople in the same year, he was introduced to literary people and married a teacher working in the Kalfayian Orphanage. He was director of the schools in Gumuldjineh and Zeitoun in 1885-1887; from 1887-1890 he was in Samson, where he founded a school. As a Hntchagian activist he travelled the provinces, but was arrested and incarcerated in the prisons of Marash and Aleppo with his wife. When he was released, he came to Constantinople and worked in the Aramian School in Kadekiugh [Kadikoy] for a year. In 1896 he escaped to Egypt where he resigned his political party membership and devoted himself to educational, literary and community work. The school he founded in Cairo prospered for four years and he published the newspapers *Punig* and *Nor Or.* He was called to the directorship of the community school in Alexandria in 1904 that he held for two years. We see him in Romania in 1907, when, after staying there for about a year, he was forced to return to Egypt, being the victim of an informer. At the

proclamation of the Constitution he drew breath in Constantinople, entering the teaching and journalism professions. He continued publishing *Punig* for a time, as well as the paper *Kaghapar* (42 editions). He was elected community assembly deputy for his birthplace. His works were mostly nationalist novels, taken from revolutionary life. *Pande Pand, Yulduzi Sassoun, Zeitouni Vreju, Tebi Yulduz, Innisoun-vets, Zeitountsi Vartabedu, Vortespan Dznoghku, Sassounen Yedku, Verchin Pertu, Demir Moushlou, Vegharavor Heros, Tiagaboudnere, Avarayri Ardzivu, Azadoutian Hamar, Ariuni Djampoun Vra, Avedaran Zeitountsineren, Pourkeren, Badmoutiun Hayots* (Vol 1), *Ariuni Tsor* (published after his death). He left, in manuscript, a volume of poems, "Lernagani Me Houshadedru", "Lerin Gouisu", "Henriat" (Voltaire). He was well versed in classical Armenian, French and Armenian history.

73. Hayg Khodjasarian was one of the prominent member of the Armenian community of Constantinople and worked on the Commission of Security with Archbishop Yegishe Turian, Haroutiun Kalfayan, Vahan Tekeyan, Haroutiun Shahrigian, Krikor Zohrab and Levon Demirjibashian. This Commission was an active one and the principal ally of Boghos Nubar Pasha's National Delegation. The Commission on Security provided the delegation with information, made suggestions, and in its turn cultivated relations with embassies, responded to their inquiries, and provided them with explanations regarding the Armenian reforms. See Zaven Patriarch, p. 23. Hayg Khodjasarian survived the Genocide and after his return he was the Chairmen of the General Assembly. *Ibid,* p. 100, He was responsible for distributing aid to needy intellectuals and their families such as Taniel Varoujan's wife, Hagop Kufedjian [Hagop Oshagan] and others in Constantinople. *Ibid,* p. 110. Zaven Patriarch describes the circumstances of the freeing of Hayg Khodjasarian. "The Charge d'affaires of the Patriarchiate, Kamer Shirinian, presented himself as a Turkophile. He had regular contacts with the Turks, enjoyed their confidence, brought me news from the government and accomplished many things. He built himself a place, helped numerous people in their official business, and benefited personally from it. I was aware of what he was doing but decided to tolerate it. His efforts after all were beneficial to various Armenians.... He saved Nerses Ohanian (member of the the Main Chancery (*Mayr Tivan*) of the National Assembly) and Arshag Alboyadjian, historian, teacher and author. He also succeeded in getting Hayg Khodjasarian to return from his place of exile." *Ibid,* p. 121.

74. Yervant Odian was born in 1869. He was a famous political satirist, prolific writer, and author of several dozen works. He survived exile. In a

letter dated January 23, 1919 to Arshag Chobanian he wrote, "I am alive after an unimaginable three and a half year ordeal. I was driven to Der Zor and even further into the Mesopotamia desert, until El Busera between the Euphrates and Kochari, where Ezegel dreamt of his visions." Yervant Odian, "Letters," Publication of the Museum of Literature and Art, Yerevan, 199, p. 244. See *Haygagan Hamaynagidaran*. After his return he published "The number 17 spy" which chronicled the events of the most tragic period of the Armenian History, 1913-1918, the preparation and the execution of the Armenian Genocide fictionalized but based on real events. This novel is 1220 pages. One of the historical relationships portrayed in the book prominently is the between Talaat and Krikor Zohrab. Odian was republished in Soviet Armenia many times. His six volume works were published in 1960. His work named *Unger Panchouni* is a political satire which could be considered the novel of the century. He revealed the inner workings of Armenian political parties. His memoirs of the Genocide were recently translated into English, Yervant Odian, *Accursed Years: My Exile and Return from Der Zor, 1914-1919,* translated from the original Armenian by Ara Stepan Melkonian with an introduction by Krikor Beledian, London: Gomidas Institute, 2009.

75. Dr. Avedis Nakkashian, a much respected medical doctor. He survived the Genocide and returned to Constantinople. See Zaven Patriarch, p. 66.

76. Pailag (Jacques Saiabalian). (Autobiography). I was born in Konya in June 1880 and received my primary education there. I attended the Berberian school in 1896 then the American school in Izmir for two years, after which I entered the world of commerce. Returning to my birthplace in 1904, I became translator for the British consul there for 5 years, during which time I acted as his deputy for a year and a half. Returning to Constantinople in 1909, I was appointed the director of the journal "Shehbal". My first article, a satirical piece, appeared in "Sourhantag". I then contributed to other Armenian newspapers, journals and yearbooks published in Constantinople. I published my poetry, a sort of correspondence, under the nom-de-plume "V", addressed to the person who is now my wife. My works: "Arachin Sere" (a novel from my school life), "Nerashkharh", "Potser Yev Eng[eroutiun]." (a satirical pamphlet) and an extensive report called "Ayriakhnam-Vorpakhnam" when I was a member of that committee (1911-1912). I'm minded to publish my poems in one volume, "Selected Pages From H. Heine's Works", as well as Conan-Doyle's novel "The Great Shadow" (Napoleon). As a provincial, I've had a great love of hunting. My favourite authors: Rostand,

Lamartine, De Renier, Silvester etc, from whose works I have a few translations.Pailag was elected deputy from his birthplace. See Teotig, p. 42.

77. Arshag Schmavonian was a lawyer and the dragoman of the American Embassy in Constantinople. He worked very closely with Henry Morgenthau, the American Ambassador to Turkey (1913-16). Morgenthau was careful not to show his close relations with the Patriarchate. According to Zaven Patriarch "through him details of the [Armenian] tragedy reached the United states government, and the American Red Cross started sending aid." Zaven Patriarch, p. p. 99.

78. Armenag Shahmouradyan, was born in Moush, 1878. He was a student of Komitas and a famous singer who performed throughout Europe.

79. Henry Morgentau, *United States Diplomacy on the Bosphorous: the Diaries of Ambassador Morgenthau, 1913-1916* compiled with an introduction by Ara Sarafian, (London: Gomidas Institute), 2004, pp. 230-31.

80. A daily newspaper which was published in Constantinople. It was the organ of the ARF. It was closed down by the authorities and resumed publication under different names, such as *Djagadamard.* Many of the arrested intellectuals worked for or published their articles in *Azadamard* over the years.

81. *Piuzantion* was a political, cultural and scientific daily. It was published from 1896-1918 in Constantinople. Piuzant Kechian and Arshag Alboyajian were a few of its editors.

82. Yervant Odian wrote a fictionalized novel on spies of Armenian origin who worked for the Ittihadist Government. *The Number 17 Spy* was first published in Constantinople in December 1918 with a preface by the author. It was republished by The Museum of Art and Literature in Yerevan in 2000.

83. Teodor Mendzigian. He was originally a bookkeeper in S. and K. Damadian's firm. Towards the end he founded his own trading house under Katerdje Oghlu Khan. He was a Tashnag sympathiser. See Teotig, p. 62.

84. Mikayel Shamdandjian survived Chankiri and wrote his memoirs of Chankiri which was published in 1919 in Canstatinople in the book compiled by Teotig, himself a survivor of Chankiri. Shamdandjian also translated and published in Constantinople, 1919 from the German original, Doctor Yohaness Lepsius' "The Secret Report on the Massacres of Armenia". Johaness Lepsius, the president of Near East Mission,

witnessed and reported in detail on the Armenian massacres. He sent his report to his fellow members of the mission in Germany in manuscript form. This 295 page work chronicled the events. This work was later serialized in *Zartonk* daily in Beirut.

85. Mustapha Kemal the founder of the modern Turkish state. He made every effort to stop the formation of Armenian state and with his repeated attacks on newly formed Armenian state in 1918 he reduced the size of the initial boundaries the Wilsonian Armenia which included a port on Black Sea Drabizond. The final boundaries of Armenia were shaped after Armenia joined the Soviet Union in November of 1920 in treaty of Moscow and on March 16,1921 and treaty of Kars which was held on October 13, 1921 which emerged in the wake of Soviet-Turkish negotiations.

86. Krikor Nor (Krikor Yesayan) was born in Van in 1883. He was a teacher of French and mathematic. He published poetry. He also translated works of Armenian poets. He was a member of the ARF. Teotig p. 46.

87. Miridjan Artinian. He was from Pera, and 30 years old. He was a typesetter for the *Levant Herald* newspaper. He was accused of being a Tashnag and deported to Ayash. See Teotig, p. 64.

88. Naim Sepha Effendi was the secretary who translated the coded telegram related to the killing of Krikor Zohrab on Oct. 4, 1915. The telegram had the signature of Talaat the ministry of interior. "For certain mandatory reasons the members of the parliament Krikor Zohrab Effendi of Constantinople, was entrusted to the commander of the 6th division of the army. The ministry of war requests from Ourfa Mutasaref and Euphrates site commander the paper work which was done on September 12, 1915 bearing the # of 514, to be send to Aleppo site to be completed which confirms that Krikor Zohrab Effendi was killed due to accident as indicated. To give the following investigation a veritable background assign a trustworthy official to do the work. Minister of Interior Talaat" see HMY p. 245 This document was among the documents that were bought from Naim Effendi.

89. Haroutiun Kalfayan. Born in Talas in 1870. Coming to Constantinople in 1886, he obtained his diploma from the school of law. He was a well-known Dashnak. Due to the events of 1896 he went to Bulgaria, from where he was expelled by the government with other revolutionary activists. After living in Egypt and Geneva for many years, he returned to Turkey at the proclamation of the Constitution and stayed in Izmir for a time, as a community activist. Upon his return to

Constantinople, he was appointed to the post of municipal inspector, then the chairman of the municipal council (belediye reyisi) of Makrikiugh [Makrikeoy], which he held until the very day of his deportation. His brother was the lawyer Arsen Kalfayian martyred in Gesaria [Kayseri]. See Teotig, p. 52.

90. Teacher Shahbaz was accused of distribution of military secrets with letters. In HMY, third edition, Beirut, 1987, p. 380.

91. Rashid Bey was invited back to become the mudir [the director] of Kharpert from his post in Baghdad by Talaat. He was the native of the region and he knew the land well. In his memoirs Davis recalls "one of the bloodiest roles of all in the tragedy enacted that summer" a fanatic he was intent to wipe out the Armenian population of the region. Rashid Bey also tried to get Davis to write a letter stating "that all the Armenians who had been deported or otherwise punished were guilty of some offense against the Government" Davis was convinced that while exterminating the Armenians Turkish government simultaneously was trying to cover up the crime. Leslie A. Davis to Henry Morgentau, Mamouret-ul-Aziz (Harput), Turkey, July 11, 1915, US State Department Record Group 59, 867.4016/ 127 in Ara Sarafian (comp. ed. and intro.), *United States Official Records on the Armenian Genocide, 1915-17*, London: Gomidas Institute, 2004.

92. Vertanes Papazian was born in Van in 1864 and died in Yerevan in 1920. Armenain writer, political and cultural worker, historian, literary critic, editor, educator and translator. He was one of the most educated people of his times. He spoke 14 languages, translated Tolstoy, Narimanov and others. He was the author of "Zeitountsineru Marche" [The March of Zeitountsees]. After 1889 he published a series of articles from lives of western Armenians, which later were published in two volumes "Snapshots from the lives of Diasporan Armenians" [Badgerner Spiurkahayots Kyankits]. Because of his revolutionary work, Papazian was persecuted by the Tsarist Russia, arrested three times, and fired from his work. His works were censored and many of his manuscripts were destroyed. In 1910 he was the first person to publish "Badmutyune Hayots Graganutyan Sgspits Minchev Mer Orere [The History of Armenian Literature from the Beginnings to Our Days]. He was condemned to death by the Turkish government. *Haygagan Sovedagan Hanrakidaran*, [Armenian Soviet Encyclopedia], Hereafter HSH vol. 12, p. 327-8.

93. Djemal Azmi, was condemned to death during the Trebizond trials in 1919 for his role in the Armenian massacres. From *Takvimi Vekayi* no. 3616 published 1919, as cited in Vahakn Dadrian "Armenian Genocide in

Official Turkish Records" in *Journal of Political and Military Sociology* 22 (1994), no. 1, pp. 165-171.

94. Simon Zavarian was born in 1865 in Aykebad-Tumanian region in Armenia and died in Constantinople in 1913. He is buried in Khojivank, Tbilisi. He was an Armenian political and public activist. A graduate of Petrovski University in Moscow, faculty of agriculture, from 1882-1886. He was a member of Tbilisi Armenian Narodnik group. In 1890 he founded the ARF with Kristapor Mikaelian, Stepan Zoryan (Rostom) and others. Until the end of his life, he was a member of its governing body, the Bureau. He adopted terror in the Armenian struggle to achieve nationalistic ideals. He authored studies on Yerevan Province, Kars region, and agriculture in Karabagh. HSH, vol. 3, p. 661.

Malkhas in his book *Abroumner* [Memories] remembers Simon Zavarian's first day as a master of his school in Trabizond Armenian School. "He was not what we expected. He was of medium height, with long black hair, attractive, with mildly effeminate mannerisms, a young adult with almost adolescent features... He would enter the school like a pupil who is late to his classes and would start the classes in a friendly way. What a surprise. We all sat and listened attentively to his lessons in agriculture. No more slapping or beating or kneeling. The use of the cane was not allowed in the school. " p. 72. Malkhas also remembers how Zavarian insisted that Vasburagan Armenians participates in fund-raising to arm the region, despite their dire financial circumstances (pp. 489-90). He argued that to involve the public in revolutionary ideals and movements, they have to participate with both financial and physical sacrifices. He explained that whatever is imported remains foreign and is not fully adopted by the people.

95. A caravan of Angora Armenians, consisting of 1,200 people, joined the Ayash prisoners with the orders of Atef, Deputy Mayor of Angora. They were killed 4-5 hours away in a valley.

96. The word "exclusive" is too strong. Perhaps "mainly" would be more appropriate.

97. Huguenin was Swiss.

98. The seizure of the Ottoman Bank by the Armenian revolutionaries was on August 15, 1895. Although the revolutionaries who seized the bank were allowed to leave the country, some of them returned back to Constantinople after 1908. In the aftermath of the Ottoman bank incident, an estimated 6,000 Armenians were killed by mobs who were let loose on the streets without police interference.

99. Footnote accompanying Aram Andonian's article: "For these diaries I remain grateful to Mr. Armenag Takvorof, who on August 29, 1915, was one of 127 Russian Armenian citizens, exiled from Constantinople to Angora. Seen as an undesirable by Angora city authorities, he was sent to Ayash. He was going to be freed only on September 18, 1918."

INDEX

Breinigsville, PA USA
18 February 2011
255847BV00002B/1/P